David & Tanner Glad
& Chris

from Jeff & Sara

MORNING Light

STEVE GREEN

with other members of the
EMPTY HANDS FELLOWSHIP

HARVEST HOUSE PUBLISHERS
Eugene, Oregon 97402

Unless otherwise indicated, all Scripture quotations in this book are taken from the Holy Bible, New International Version ®, Copyright © 1973,1978,1984 by the International Bible Society. Used by permission of Zondervan Publishing House. The "NIV" and "New International Version" trademarks are registered in the United States Patent and Trademark Office by International Bible Society.

Verses marked KJV are taken from the King James Version of the Bible.

Verses marked NKJV are taken from the New King James Version, Copyright © 1979, 1980, 1982 by Thomas Nelson, Inc., Publishers. Used by permission.

Verses marked TEV are taken from The Bible in Today's English Version (Good News Bible), © American Bible Society 1966, 1971, 1976. Used by permission.

Verses marked NASB are taken from the New American Standard Bible, © 1960, 1962, 1963, 1968, 1971, 1972, 1973, 1975, 1977, 1995 by The Lockman Foundation. Used by permission.

Cover by Koechel Peterson & Associates, Minneapolis, Minnesota

Author photo by Dave Pavol

MORNING LIGHT

Copyright © 1999 Steve Green Ministries
Published by Harvest House Publishers
Eugene, Oregon 97402

Library of Congress Cataloging-in-Publication Data
Morning light / Steve Green, general editor.
    p.   cm.
  ISBN 0-7369-0205-8
   1. Devotional literature, English.   2. Contemporary Christian music Texts.
  I. Green, Steve.
BV4832.2.M599   1999
242—DC21   99-28579
                                                                CIP

Printed in the United States of America.

99 00 01 02 03 04 / DH / 10 9 8 7 6 5 4 3 2

*We, of the Empty Hands,
would like to dedicate this
book to the memory of*

WILLIAM LANE,

*who in just fourteen months
changed us all for a lifetime.*

CONTENTS

I am grateful to:

Peter York, for suggesting that this book should be written.

Carolyn McCready, for diligently listening to each contributor, working to preserve the unique diversity of such a collaboration.

Terry Glaspey, for giving an amazing amount of time, energy, and loving attention to this project. It could not have been done without him. His editing was prayerful and respectful.

The Empty Hands brothers, for taking the time to give us a glimpse into the rich deposit God has placed within your lives.

STEVE GREEN

Introduction

STEVE GREEN

orning has special meaning for the Christian. Charles Spurgeon once wrote, "While the dew is on the grass, let grace drop upon the soul. Let us give to God the morning of our days and the morning of our lives." Morning points us to the Creator, giving us a daily reminder that in the beginning God created the heavens and the earth. The morning takes its orders from God and the dawn finds its place in His purpose.

It was in the cool of daybreak that God came to Adam and Eve, walking deliberately, calling to them patiently, and mercifully lifting them from their fall. God's provision for them, and promise to us through Christ, is that as the morning mist disappears with the rising of the sun, so God sweeps away our sins like a cloud.

Morning was the time for swift obedience from Abraham, Isaac, and Jacob, who responded with obedience to God as the first act of their day. Early in the morning they rose to carry out what God had commanded.

The Levitical priests were told to keep the fire on the altar from going out. Each morning they were to add firewood and rekindle the flame, giving us a picture of the daily need to awaken a renewed love for Christ. Just as there were specific sacrifices they were instructed to offer in the morning, so the start of our days should be perfumed with the fragrance of worship.

This life is filled with difficulties, trials, and suffering, but our Lord has assured us that better times are ahead. Though weeping may endure for the night, rejoicing comes in the morning. At the dawn of each new day, God reveals fresh mercies and tender compassion. As we draw near to Him, He draws near to us—to comfort and strengthen those whose hearts are wholly His. The gospel assures us that in Christ the old is gone and the new is come. Each new morning trumpets the message of salvation, reminding us that we are recipients of God's grace.

The turning point of history, the resurrection of Jesus Christ from the dead, was also a morning event. And each morning we hear the joyful strains of God's summons, "Arise, shine; for your light has come, and the glory of the LORD has risen upon you" (Isaiah 60:1).

One of the highlights of my week is the Thursday noon prayer meeting of the Empty Hands Fellowship. Young and old, this diverse group of brothers gathers to lay hold of the horns of the altar. I had been asked to write a devotional book to accompany my latest album, a collection of songs that could be used for morning devotions. But as I sat listening to the men of Empty Hands pray one Thursday, it dawned on me that *these* were the ones who should write this book. In a fragile, yet confident, voice, 75-year-old Bob Smith lifted his prayer toward heaven. It seemed to me that if I had opened my eyes, I could have reached out my hand and touched the Lord. Lifelong passion and faith, forged in the secret place of private worship, found expression as one man after another called upon the name of the Lord.

Many of these wonderful men are tucked away from view, hidden in ministries that few will ever hear about. What I have discovered, however, is that God has deposited some of His richest treasures in hard to find places. Gold, silver, and precious stones are beneath the earth's surface and must be mined. So, here, with great joy, I offer to you a treasure I have discovered—wrapped up in the lives of these friends, the Empty Hands Fellowship.

The Empty Hands Story

very Thursday at noon, they gather together to pray. When twelve o'clock rolls around, they find their seats in the old wooden pews at First Missionary Baptist Church, a small African-American congregation just east of downtown Franklin, Tennessee. They greet each other warmly, without pretension. Some are dressed formally, with suits and ties. Others have thrown on a sweatshirt, with the gym their next stop. As they find a seat, there are plenty of hugs and abundant laughter.

Briefly, they share prayer requests: personal struggles, issues that their churches are facing, and concerns for the community, especially for the young people. As an older pastor shares his concern for wayward youth who are growing up without hope, you can see many heads nodding in agreement. A younger pastor then shares a very personal concern. You know that he must trust these other men to open up his heart with such vulnerability. There is no macho posturing going on here. As one of the men says, "There is no hurt that

I cannot take to any of these men. With them, admitting my need doesn't make me any less a man." This kind of trust is one of the hallmarks of Empty Hands Fellowship, the name they have given this weekly gathering of pastors and church leaders.

The name "Empty Hands" reflects their philosophy. They understand that they have nothing to bring to God except a broken and contrite heart. They know the importance of recognizing their total dependence upon Him. They recognize that they must come before Him with empty hands, without any agenda other than that of allowing God to use them. And they are learning that opening up to God is the first step to opening up to others. Because this group is so ethnically diverse, this kind of openness is not something you might expect. But it can be found among these men. There is no claim here of color blindness. Everyone recognizes the cultural differences that arise from race and economic background, but these differences are seen as a cause for celebration rather than suspicion. Each man is learning that you can discover a lot about yourself when you see yourself through the eyes of another.

Along with trust, the other hallmark of Empty Hands is prayer—fervent, concerted, purposeful prayer. And when these men begin to pray, the presence of God becomes palpable in the room. You can sense the depth of their hearts as they pour out simple and passionate prayers to the Lord. The hour seems to fly by as they all occupy themselves with the serious business of prayer.

The men who gather include an assortment of pastors, church leaders, and individuals involved in other kinds of ministries. They include Caucasians and African-Americans, as well as a Hispanic pastor and a Native American musician. Two of them make a living by sharing the gospel through music: Michael Card and Steve Green. While several have little or no formal education, one of them (Bill Lane, who died of a brain aneurysm just days after completing his devotions for this book) held a Ph.D. and was one of the nation's most respected New Testament scholars and an author of several highly esteemed Bible commentaries. These men come from all kinds of backgrounds, from the African-American pastor who admits that before his encounter with this group he would not even speak to a white man unless absolutely necessary to a man who has built a cross-cultural ministry around the idea of reaching out to the underprivileged. In fact, he took the call so seriously that he moved his family out of their comfortable middle-class neighborhood and into one of the underprivileged areas of Franklin, a neighborhood known for drug-dealing and gang crimes.

The men of Empty Hands freely admit to being kind of a motley crew. It's hard to find much that these men hold in common other than their love for Jesus Christ. But that love is strong enough to spill over into a heartfelt commitment to each other. And out of that commitment has arisen the desire to work together for the good of their community. They have cooperated to sponsor a city-wide tent meeting that will draw together all the ethnically diverse congregations of Franklin and are researching a job-training program designed to help young men and women get off the streets and into productive occupations. They are also committed to support a children's clinic and a drug rehabilitation center.

But Empty Hands Fellowship has never lost sight of its primary vision of meeting together to pray and demonstrate real love for one another. Although its numbers have grown, its focus has not changed. Prayer and relationship are at the heart of what they are all about. As Denny Denson, pastor of First Missionary Baptist, says, "We're not trying to be a social group; we're a group of men developing intimate relationships. If we meet one another on the street or in the local Wal-Mart, we are quick to share a hug." Or, in the words of Scott Roley, "We are Christian men who love one another and pray for one another."

This kind of love hasn't come easily. Some of the guys have had a lot to get past: racial issues, economic issues, differences in education, and theological background. Sometimes the biggest struggles can be with unintentional thoughtlessness.

Scott remembers how he and Denny first met. Scott was one of the pastors of the large Christ Community Church, the biggest church in Franklin and one made famous by the fact that so many Christian recording artists call it home. He had planned a work party for the youth of Christ Community, who went into an underprivileged neighborhood (where Denny pastors) to clean out front yards, repaint houses, and offer financial assistance. They had such an impact that Denny began to hear about it from his neighbors. "Yeah," people of the neighborhood would say, comparing the two churches, "you help us with the occasional electric bill, but they repainted my house!" He could not help but be a little annoyed at the comparison of what his small congregation could do to help local residents and the ample monetary resources available through Christ Community. Also, he couldn't help but wonder why they had not asked for his help and cooperation in this ministry. After all, they were doing their work right in his "front yard." Was it another instance of what happens in so many communities across the country—where white and African-American churches exist side by side, believing the same gospel, worshiping the same Lord, and yet having very little to do with one another? Why hadn't Scott even bothered to make contact with him?

When Denny shared his frustration with another African-American pastor, the word got back to Scott, who felt an immediate conviction that he wanted to do something to amend the situation. Although his intentions had been good, he realized that he had offended a brother and overlooked his brother's ministry. He went right to Denny's church, climbed the front steps, and met Denny coming down the aisle of the church. Scott blurted out, "I'm sorry," and then the two men embraced and wept. It was a moment neither will soon forget.

Denny was quick to reply, "You don't owe me an apology." Any animosity he may have carried in his heart had been melted by the Holy Spirit. He realized that this was the answer to a prayer he had prayed for years. The tears they shed together that day became the seeds of the Empty Hands Fellowship. They realized that other pastors had been meeting in small multi-racial groups, so they all joined together to pool their resources and pursue a unified vision...and the Lord has richly blessed the undertaking.

The same kind of openness that Denny and Scott shared that day has continued to be a mark of the Fellowship. The idea was not to form a club or a clique, but to make a commitment to each other. The goal is not appeasing guilt or racial reconciliation. It is about really *being* the body of Christ, about showing visible care for one another, and about "doing life" together, as one man so memorably put it. Steve Green reminds us that "distance causes separation. The glue that holds it all together is love. Love makes you value and respect the hearts of others."

One thing that all the men agree on: They wait with empty hands and open hearts. They are waiting to see what God is going to do in their midst. And He is certainly moving. The treasure they share together is something that each can take back to his own congregation. God is doing a significant work here. And it is all founded upon two things: prayer and love for one another.

This book of devotions contains the writings of twelve of the men who are involved in Empty Hands. Taken together, these devotions give evidence of the diversity of the group. The variety of writing styles and the wide-ranging content of the messages reflect each man's own background and personal spiritual journey. But they all share in common a love for the Scriptures, a dedication to the Lord Jesus Christ, and a commitment to one another. We stand to learn a lot from both their lives and their writings.

AWAKEN

Words by Steve Green
Music by Steve Green
and Phil Naish

Wake up sleeping soul
The gift of light unfolds
Slowly the night gives way
Before the dawning day

Shine in, O Morning Light
Chase back the shades of night
Fill my heart with a song
Silence has reigned too long

I will awaken the dawn
Be the first voice of praise with a song
Till the morning joins in and creation begins
To awake to the sound of this song

High as the heav'ns above
So great is the Father's love
Love unconditionally
Rejoicing over me

I will awaken the dawn
Be the first voice of praise with a song
Till the morning joins in and creation begins
To awake to the sound of this song

Yo quiero cantar con felicidad
(*I want to sing with joy*)
Porque Tu renuevas mi ser, al amanecer
(*For You renew my soul in the morning*)

Alma, despierta ya (*Wake up, soul*)
Huye la oscuridad (*The darkness flees*)
Venga a la Santa Luz (*Come to the holy light*)
De El Señor Jesus (*Of Jesus the Lord*)

I will awaken the dawn
Be the first voice of praise with a song
Till the morning joins in and creation begins
To awake to the sound of this song

An award-winning Christian musician, Steve Green has touched numerous lives through his music and testimony. In addition to adding countless classic songs to the church's repertoire, such as "People Need the Lord," "Find Us Faithful," and "God and God Alone," he has written two devotional books. Steve has a heart for missions and has performed all over the world. In the devotions he has written, you'll glimpse the heart of a man who is intimate with God and articulate in the sharing of his faith.

Stirring Up Our Affections

Revelation 2:4

STEVE GREEN

Ever since Adam and Eve's fall in the garden of Eden, deterioration has taken its toll on everything around us. If farmland is left unattended, weeds will overtake the crops and spoil the harvest. If we do not exercise our bodies, our muscles begin to atrophy, our heart is weakened, and we experience a loss of energy and alertness. If our minds are not stimulated and disciplined, we can forget even familiar things very quickly. The effects of this deterioration are also evident in our spiritual lives. The hymn writer expressed it this way, "Prone to wander, Lord I feel it; prone to leave the God I love." Haven't you lamented the times your heart was cold and your affection for Christ has diminished? If so, you are not alone. The lifelong struggle

21

of every follower of Jesus is to maintain a vital, intimate love relationship with Him.

After the Israelites set up the Old Testament Tabernacle as God had prescribed, the priests were ordained and began their ministry. On the day of consecration, fire came out from the presence of the Lord and lit the altar's fire. From then on, the priests were to keep the fire burning continuously, never letting it go out (Leviticus 9:24; 6:12). In the same way, God is the author of our salvation, the One who calls us and makes us His own. Yet we are to earnestly seek Him and hold on to the hope we have received. This demands great care and attention, for the peril of hardening our hearts and drifting away from the Lord is ever present. The apostle Paul told the Corinthian believers that he was afraid they would be deceived by the serpent's cunning and somehow be led astray from a sincere and pure devotion to Christ. We are in danger of the same thing. So how can we stir up our affections for God? What steps can we take to keep our spiritual fervor alive?

Bob was standing in line to greet me after one of my concerts. I saw him coming. He had a crew cut, a barrel chest, and a rugged ex-marine look. Although he was now in his sixties, he still looked intimidating. As we shook hands, I asked Bob how he was doing. "Oh, all right, I guess, but I just need to do better and try harder," he answered gruffly. In his voice I detected the weariness of a lifelong attempt to perform perfectly. We spoke briefly, then I asked permission to pray for him. As I closed my eyes, I felt the love that God had for this man. I could almost see the Father's tears, longing for Bob to enter His rest. I began to express God's affection and described

His unconditional acceptance, how instead of being angry and demanding, keeping us at arm's length till we perform correctly, God lavishes kindness on us and accepts us in Christ. Somewhere during the prayer I felt Bob's shoulder begin to shake. Then I heard a sniffle. By the end, he was weeping freely. What happened? The grace and relief of the gospel had caught him by surprise. Expecting to hear a "shape up or ship out" scolding, the Lord came to him instead with tenderness and love. God's kindness melted his heart.

How long had it been since you have been warmed by the reassurance of God's love? Maybe everyone else only accepts you on the basis of your performance, but God lavishes love on you without reserve. Paul's prayer for the Ephesians was that, being rooted and established in love, they would have power "to grasp how wide and long and high and deep is the love of Christ, and to know this love that surpasses knowledge" (Ephesians 3:18,19).

Frederick Lehman expressed God's love this way,

> Could we with ink the ocean fill,
> And were the skies of parchment made,
> Were every stalk on earth a quill,
> And every man a scribe by trade,
> To write the love of God above
> Would drain the ocean dry.
> Nor could the scroll contain the whole
> Though stretched from sky to sky.

Unlike others, the Lord is never far off. He does not withdraw into silence when we offend, nor does He lash out in retaliation when we disobey. Rather, divine love flows from infinite joy and perfect bliss. Those who are adopted into His family through faith in Christ are the objects of His favor, the apple of His eye, the delight of His heart. How can your affection for Christ be renewed? Let His love blow across the embers of your heart, rekindling your love.

It is important to remember that the coldness of our hearts is not some trivial matter, nor must we suspect that our Lord is indifferent about our loss of love. In His letter to the church of Ephesus, (Revelation 2:4,5) Jesus speaks a stern word of rebuke. While commending them for the good things they did, He did not neglect to point out where they had gone wrong. Amid all the right things they were doing there was a sin that had to be addressed. They had left their first love. The degree of fervency had diminished.

God lavishes LOVE ON YOU without reserve

Their initial response to salvation, the joy of forgiveness, the bright hope of heaven, had caused their hearts to well up in loving adoration, but somewhere along the way something had changed. Now they were serving diligently, working faithfully, but loving dutifully. They were polite and respectful, but lacking in earnest affection.

On our way to church one Sunday morning, we had a family discussion on this same topic. One of my children was not at all happy about sitting through our worship service. In fact, I could feel their attitude seeping over from the back seat and spoiling the sweetness of the morning. "Do you think we're doing God a favor by attending church this morning?" I asked. "Do you really imagine that God is watching us from heaven and saying, 'I know this is no fun and you really don't want to be here, but thanks for making the effort, it means a lot to Me'? Do you suppose He wants our time and not our hearts? What if I took your mom out for a date to a nice restaurant and during the meal she said, 'Honey, what a nice evening. Why did you do this?' and I were to respond coolly, 'I thought I should service our relationship.' Wouldn't that be offensive? Mom doesn't want my 'have to' time, she wants time that flows from a desire to be with her. How much more do you think our Lord is pleased with our 'want to' time? It would be better to turn around now and not even go to church, than to sin against God by our lack of love." How well I can identify with the frailty of my children, for I have also had the same attitude many times.

The Lord Jesus counseled the Ephesian believers to remember the height from which they had fallen, to exercise their memories and compare their present condition to the former. How much peace, strength, and comfort they had lost. What a burden the duty of religion was without the inspiration of fervent love. They must repent and grieve over the great disparity between the infinitely tender love of Christ and their declining response. Repentance means retracing each step back to the place where the first wrong step was taken, and humbly seeking the right way again.

There was one more thing Jesus told them. "Do the things you did at first." He was suggesting the need to begin again, seeking to revive and recover their first zeal. Maybe they could remember the evidence of first love, the things they did when motivated by an ardent affection for Christ. The joy of abiding in His presence, the eagerness to serve, the indifference to earthly concerns, a genuine love for others, and a grieving over what offends Him.

Even as I write this, I'm recalling the time Christ's love captured my heart. I remember missed meals, forgotten while caught up in prayer, and the eager anticipation of opening His Word. I remember weeping for those who were broken and didn't know my God. The question I must ask myself is "how is my love for Christ today?"

Perhaps your heart has been stirred by the thought that God delights in you; that He looks on you with kind affection. Or, you may have been convicted that you have left your first love and sense that the Lord is calling you to return to Him with all your heart. One of the songs I often sing when I'm alone is a prayer asking the Lord to revive and restore a passion for Christ. Maybe you would want to pray it with me now.

> "More love to Thee, O Christ,
> More love to Thee
> Hear now the prayer I make
> On bended knee.
> This is my earnest plea,
> More love O Christ to Thee.
> More love to Thee,
> More love to Thee."

A Fixed Heart
Psalm 57:7

STEVE GREEN

David's words in Psalm 57:7 do not seem all that extraordinary or remarkable until we realize when and where they were spoken. King Saul, whose jealousy had been aroused by David's military triumph over the Philistines, knew for certain that God had rejected him as king and was raising up David to rule in his place. Saul was intent, therefore, on getting rid of the competition. Already he had tried twice to pin David to the wall with a spear. Now, being told that David was in the desert of Maon, Saul set out with an army of three thousand men to destroy his enemy.

Surely David, the brave warrior, the giant-slayer, and the lion-killer was not afraid of Saul. But what do you suppose David was doing? Maybe he was devising a brilliant battle plan. Perhaps he was taking up positions in the rocky crags, ready to pounce and attack. Well, not exactly. Are you ready for this? David and his men were hiding in the back of a cave!

Suddenly there's a hush. "Look!" David's soldiers whispered. There was Saul at the mouth of the cave, relieving himself. Excitement ran through David's men. "This is the day the Lord spoke of when He said to you, 'I will give your enemy into your hands.'" Here was his chance! All he had to do was quietly sneak up behind Saul and...it would be over. David did creep up behind Saul, close enough to have killed him. Instead, he simply cut off a piece of the garment Saul had laid aside. Then he went back and rebuked his men for even suggesting that he should lift his hand against the Lord's anointed one. Was he really hiding in fear, or was there a remarkable confidence in what he did? What made David act so nobly? What held him steady in the moment of danger and temptation? David could act as he did because his heart was fixed.

That same word, "fixed" is used 77 times in the Old Testament. It means established, prepared, ready, stable, set, faithful, certain, and ordered. It's the word David uses in his petition, "Oh, that my ways were steadfast in obeying your decrees," and "Direct my footsteps according to your word"(Psalm 119:5,133).

I'm sure David drew confidence from remembering the powerful way he had been called. God sent Samuel to Jesse's house in Bethlehem to make a sacrifice and anoint Saul's successor, who would come from among Jesse's sons. Surely, Eliab, the oldest, tallest, and best-looking son, was the one the Lord was after. Instead, the Lord spoke in Samuel's ear,

"Do not consider his appearance or his height, for I have rejected him. The LORD does not look at the things man looks at. Man looks at the outward appearance, but the LORD looks at the heart" (1 Samuel 16:7). Jesse had six of his other sons appear before Samuel to see if any of them would be chosen.

"Are these all the sons you have?" Samuel asked. Well no, came the answer, there was still David, the youngest son, but he was out tending the sheep. The kid was so unimportant that even with a sacrifice and feast about to take place at home, no one had bothered to call him in. He was the least likely to be chosen. Yet, Samuel would not sit down till David had arrived from the fields. As soon as he came in, the Lord said, "Rise and anoint him; he is the one." In an instant, David was designated the next king of Israel.

Can you imagine all the questions he must have had? When would this take place? How long would he have to wait? His head must have been spinning. How would he know when the time was right?

What David could not have known was that it would be almost ten years before he would take Saul's place as king. During these important years, he would learn to wait on the Lord and trust God to fulfill all He had promised. Somewhere during those ten years David finds himself in a cave, being hunted like an animal by an angry King Saul. Yet by this time his confidence in God's provision has grown strong. He has faced Goliath and seen that the battle belongs to the Lord. He has been spared from Saul's pursuit and attacks. He has learned to cast himself on the Lord and cry out to Him for help. Although he's hiding in a cave, David's heart is so steady that he can say, "In you my soul takes refuge" (Psalm 57:1). He remembers the day Samuel anointed him as the next king and is certain that God will accomplish all He has promised.

There's another reason his heart is fixed. Not only does he have confidence in the promises of God and His unchanging nature, but also God has allowed David to be stripped of everything else that might get in the way, so that his heart can be fixed on God alone.

Sarah (not her real name) wrote me a letter detailing her hour of testing. As a mother of young children and the wife of a caring husband, Sarah's life was full and blessed. Then her world began to fall apart. At first, the irritation in her throat seemed more like a nuisance. It must be a passing virus or an allergic reaction, she thought. Yet the soreness persisted and the pain increased. After testing, the doctors called her in for a consultation. How do you tell a vibrant young mother that she has cancer of the throat? Over the next few months, Sarah's life changed dramatically. There was one particular moment she highlighted for me. Eating had become extremely painful. Her diet consisted mostly of liquids, with only the occasional possibility of a few soft foods. Any swallowing was painful. Weeks passed slowly and painfully. After days of no solid food, she yearned for just a small piece of cracker. She savored the small bite, chewing it very carefully. Yet as she swallowed, the roughness of the cracker tore open the tender membrane in her throat, causing a fresh flow of blood and intense pain. Falling to the floor, Sarah cried out to

God in agony, "Lord, I can't even take one bite of food! The pain is unbearable. I don't know how much more I can endure." There, on the floor, in utter desperation and brokenness, something holy took place. The Lord surrounded her with love and compassion. In tearful adoration she prayed, "Lord, You are enough! If I never have another bite of food, or a day without pain, or never live to see my children grow up, You are enough. If I have You, I have all that I need."

What does your cave look like? Where are you hiding in your hour of difficulty? Does God really allow His children to get to such a desperate place? I mean, can it really be God's purpose to get us to the back of the cave, with no way out?

Very reverently and with much trembling, may I suggest that God, in His kindness and mercy, sometimes allows us to come to the end of ourselves so we realize that He is enough. Then, when our hearts are fixed on Him alone, we can say with David, "My heart is fixed, O God. My heart is fixed. For great is your love, reaching the heavens; your faithfulness reaches to the skies."

Dressed for the Day

1 Thessalonians 5:8

STEVE GREEN

"Good Mooorning," my mother would sing out as she swept open the curtains, turned on the light, and gave my brothers and me a mouth-watering description of what was waiting on the breakfast table. "Oooh," we would moan, covering our eyes from the blinding brightness and attempting to stifle her cheerfulness. It never worked. She loved the morning. Nothing could diminish the unrestrained joy she experienced with the beginning of each new day.

Wouldn't you know it. I married a woman who shares the same enthusiasm. Marijean goes to sleep anticipating the daybreak. Now it's my son who groans as his mom opens the blinds, describes the splendor of the day, and tries to lure him downstairs to breakfast.

What about you? How do you handle the morning? "I'm not a morning person," you may reply. "I don't even like to talk until after my first cup of coffee." "And remember," you may add with a solemn air, "the Scriptures have a warning for people like you: 'He that blesseth his friend with a loud voice, rising early in the morning, it shall be counted a curse to him!'" (Proverbs 27:14). Well, that's not exactly what the verse means, but you see the point.

Whether you greet the morning with a smile or with a moan, I've got news for you. We are children of the day. We belong to the kingdom of light. Ephesians 5:8 reminds us that once we were darkness, that our hearts were darkened by sin, ignorance, and unbelief. Yet now, we have become light in the Lord. He has rescued us from the dominion of darkness by making His light to shine in our hearts, giving us the "light of the knowledge of the glory of God in the face of Christ" (2 Corinthians 4:6). This world is a dark place, and the spiritual forces of evil wage war against the King of Light and His subjects. Under the cloak of darkness, sin festers and vice multiplies. Many cities come alive at night, but what takes place in them is most often shameful. Even a beer commercial boasts that the night belongs to them, suggesting that fulfillment is to be found in unrestrained passions.

But we are children of the day, remember? While the world sleeps, unaware of the approaching day of the Lord (which will come upon them as a thief in the night), we are to be sober minded, vigilant, watchful, and alert. While the world slips into the slumber of death, plunging headlong into depravity, we are to guard against all that would dull our senses and lull us to sleep.

What does the Apostle Paul advise? How are we to be prepared? In 1 Thessalonians 5:8, he admonishes us to get dressed for the day by putting on the spiritual armor of faith, love, and hope. The pieces of armor he prescribes are the breastplate and helmet, which protect the most vital parts of the soldier's body, the head and the heart.

The first is faith. How does faith protect us? Faith is critical because it is the means by which we believe the gospel, it is the hand with which we grasp the gift of salvation. Faith casts itself upon the Word of God, trusting

Love keeps A TENDER EYE ON the Master

completely in all God has said. Faith leads us to the place of perfect rest and confidence, certain of our calling, our justification, the forgiveness of our sin, and our adoption as sons and daughters. When the enemy's flaming arrows fly at us, faith extinguishes them by holding to the truth of God's Word. The light of Scripture uncovers every lie and exposes all deceit. Have you put on the breastplate of faith this morning?

Another means of protection is love. A heart inflamed with love for God will not doubt His goodness, even in the most difficult of times. Though the enemy may level accusations against the Lord, tempting us to doubt His character, love says, "though he slay me, yet will I trust in him"

(Job 13:15). Love keeps a tender eye on the Master, watchful lest anything spoil the sweetness of our fellowship with Him. It adds cheerfulness to obedience and delight to duty, keeping us in the safety of God's commands.

Lastly, we are to put on the hope of salvation as a helmet. This hope is not at all like the weak, wishful thinking of worldly longings. No, this is a joyful, confident expectation, based upon our resurrected, living Lord. Through Him we have been given new birth into a living hope. While for most people, "hope deferred makes the heart sick" (Proverbs 13:12), the believer's hope is fueled by God's promises. Like Abraham, who believed against all hope, confident that God had power to do all He had said, we too, remain joyful in hope. Instead of diminishing with time, our confidence increases. How is this possible? It is possible because God has poured His love into our hearts by the Holy Spirit, giving us a deposit and guarantee of what is to come. The Spirit Himself testifies with our spirits that we are God's dearly loved children. Even though we do not see our Lord, we are filled with an "inexpressible and glorious joy" (1 Peter 1:8,9), for we are receiving the goal of our faith, the salvation of our souls. God gives us daily reassurance and comfort through His Word, teaching and encouraging us to continue in this hope.

Can you see how essential this armor is? Not only are we warned about the dangers that surround us, we are also given the means to be protected. Not only are we told about the outcome and look forward to our Lord's return, but the God of hope has given us hope as an anchor for our souls to hold us steady till the end. As you start your day, be sure to put on your armor. Get dressed for the day!

Acceptable Praise

Hebrews 13:15

STEVE GREEN

What comes to mind when you hear the word "praise"? In my travels I've been in almost every kind of church service, from liturgical recitations spoken in hushed awe to emotionally charged expressions of passionate familiarity.

So, which of these two describes praise? Maybe it is somewhere in the middle. Obviously, there is much discussion about the best way to worship, and there is also a good measure of smug certainty that our own way is the right way. Unfortunately, the formal, liturgical worshiper can often view the more expressive brethren as flippant and irreverent, while the hand-raising, chorus-singing worshipers can look down on the others as frigid and lifeless.

Do you remember the account of King David's attempt to bring the Ark of the Covenant back to Jerusalem (2 Samuel 6)? Now that David was firmly established as king, his heart was drawn to honor God and restore the ark to its place of prominence in Zion. With thirty thousand elders, nobles, and leaders (not counting the multitude that followed), David set out to retrieve the ark from the house of Abinadab. The ark was placed on a new cart and pulled along by oxen. Abinadab's sons, Uzzah and Ahio, were most familiar with the ark, for it had remained in their house for some time. While Ahio walked in front, probably guiding the oxen, Uzzah stayed next to the cart, watchful of the ruts and bumps along the way that could upset their precious cargo.

"David and the whole house of Israel were celebrating with all their might before the Lord, with songs and with harps, lyres, tambourines, sistrums and cymbals" (2 Samuel 6:5). Suddenly, the oxen stumbled and Uzzah reached out his hand, taking hold of the ark to steady it. The Lord's anger burned against him and he was struck down. Uzzah died on the spot.

Now wait a minute! Don't you think that celebrating with all their might would count for something? These people were sincere and their worship was "before the Lord." It wasn't just a carnal expression of riotous exuberance. How could it be that, while they were celebrating and offering God their most energetic praise, God was displeased? What was the problem? First of all, the ark was not to be transported on a cart as the Philistines had done, but was to be carried on poles by the Levites. And though Uzzah was a Levite, according to Numbers 4:15, they were not to touch the ark under penalty of death. David later acknowledged this error, "It was because you, the Levites, did not bring it up the first time that the Lord our God broke out in anger against us. We did not inquire of him about how to do it in the prescribed way" (1 Chronicles 15:13).

The Lord was teaching here that good intentions do not justify wrong actions. Worship that feels right may not *be* right. God has a prescribed way for us to praise Him.

First, our praise must be "through Jesus Christ." Apart from Him, I am miserably alienated from God. Do I really understand that all my good works, all my attempts at obedience, all my prayers and songs are unacceptable apart from the Lord Jesus? Oh, how the gospel brings blessed relief to our hopeless condition. Through the death of Christ, God reconciled me to Himself and now accepts me as holy, without blemish, and free from accusation. What an astounding thing! The basis of my relationship with God is forever rooted in Christ. He is my high priest, the One who made the sacrifice for my sin. He is my righteousness, the One who fulfilled all the requirements of the Law on my behalf. He is my intercessor, the One who pleads my case before Holy God. All that I offer to God is acceptable in and through Him.

Isn't that encouraging? Have you ever felt that you just couldn't praise God as well as other people, sing as well, or be as free in your expression of worship? Cheer up! If you come to God through Christ, your offerings are perfectly accepted.

Your songs are beautiful, your words of praise are treasured, and your heartfelt gratitude rises toward heaven as incense.

Second, we must remember that praise is a sacrifice, a giving of something that is valuable. Through Malachi, the Lord rebuked the Israelites for showing contempt for His name. "How have we shown contempt?" they asked. One way was by placing defiled food on the altar, and bringing blind, lame, and sick animals for sacrifice (Malachi 1:6-8). G. Campbell Morgan suggests that although sacrilege is generally interpreted as taking something that belongs to God and using it profanely, according to this text, sacrilege is also taking something and giving it to God when it means nothing to me. Matthew Henry continues the thought.

> If we worship God ignorantly, and without under-
> standing, we bring the blind for sacrifice. If we do
> it carelessly, and without consideration, if we are
> cold, and dull, and dead, in it, we bring the sick.
> If we do not make heart-work of it, if we suffer
> vain thoughts and distractions to lodge within us,
> we bring the torn.

These are strong words, but a good reminder of the reverence that God is due. I have sometimes caught myself singing thoughtlessly and offering prayers that were repetition, approaching God with coldness of heart. Day after day, I must ask the Lord to magnify Himself in my sight. I need to see His matchless beauty again, so that my offerings are a fitting response to His great worth.

Finally, praise that is acceptable is the fruit of our lips, evidence of hearts warmed by the reality of an intimate, vital relationship with Christ.

William Temple offers these thoughts:

> Worship is the submission of all our nature to God,
> The quickening of conscience by His holiness,
> The nourishment of mind by His truth,
> The purifying of imagination by His beauty,
> The opening of the heart to His love,
> And the submission of will to His purpose.
> All this, gathered up in adoration,
> Is the greatest of human expressions of which we are
>   capable.

Heavenly Father, would You awaken our hearts to the glory and splendor of Your grace? Make us alive to Your Spirit and fully aware of the infinite perfections of Your nature. Then, Lord, conquer and overpower our hearts with Your goodness and love, so that our praise will rise to You in flames of deep affection. Through Jesus Christ our Lord. Amen.

ALL THAT YOU SAY

Words by Steve Green
Music by Wes King

All that You say and reveal
All You command and conceal
All of Your Word here for me
All that You say is all that I need.

Blessed are the ones who listen
Blessed are the ones who hear
Speak Lord, while I am waiting
Speak while my heart is near.

All that is true, all that's right
All that is pure, radiant light
All of Your heart here for me
All that You say is all I need.

Blessed are the ones who listen
Blessed are the ones who hear
Speak Lord, while I am waiting
Speak while my heart is near.

Thy Word is a lamp to my feet
And a light unto my path.

Blessed are the ones who listen
Blessed are the ones who hear
Speak Lord, while I am waiting
Speak while my heart is near.

Blessed are the ones who listen
Blessed are the ones who hear
Speak Lord, while I am waiting
Speak while my heart is near.

Speak Lord, while I am waiting.

Chris Williamson is the senior pastor of Strong Tower Bible Church, a church that attracts members from a variety of racial and economic backgrounds. A graduate of Liberty University and Liberty Baptist Theological Seminary, Chris has also recorded two albums with the gospel rap group, Transformation Crusade. One of the things that draws people to Strong Tower is Chris' relevant biblical teaching, delivered with a streetwise sense of humor that you'll surely notice in these devotions.

Not By Bread Alone

Matthew 4:4

REV. CHRIS WILLIAMSON

The words, "You are what you eat," sprawl across most high school cafeteria walls as an incentive to persuade students to eat healthy. However, while going through the serving lines, students generally resolve that chocolate chip cookies, soda pop, and ice cream are more inviting than the day's "mystery meat." Nutritionists have proven that our diet, whether good or poor, has a direct effect on how we behave. Spiritually speaking, the same principle is true. What we "eat" from the Word of God has a direct effect on how we behave as Christians.

As important as food is to our survival, Jesus reveals that there is something more essential than food itself. He said "Man shall not live by bread alone but by every word that proceeds from the mouth of God" (Matthew 4:4). This means that spiritual nourishment is more important than physical nourishment, just as spiritual training is more important than physical training (1 Timothy 4:7,8). Physical food or bread, is a *luxury*, while spiritual food, which is the Word of God, is an *essential*. If breakfast is said to be the most important meal of the day because it fuels us to get going, how much more important is our devotional "breakfast" in the Word to get our day started right? Wow, talk about the "Breakfast of Champions"! God's Word does more than give fuel, it gives life (John 6:63).

Colossians 3:16 says, "Let the word of Christ dwell in you richly." The Word of God will be at home with us to the extent that we are *at home* with the Word of God. According to John 15:7, our goal should be to abide in the Word, so that the Word abides in us and flows through us. The Word will move into every room of our hearts (Hebrews 4:12), and with the assistance of the Holy Spirit, it will transform, redecorate, and remodel us from the inside out.

The spiritual man is to be fed and renewed through the Word day by day (2 Corinthians 4:16). Christ said, "My food is to do the will of Him who sent me, and to finish His work" (John 4:34 NKJV). What is your food today? Do you know the will of Him who sent you? His will is found is His Word.

One of the distinctive elements of African-American cuisine is "soul food." Soul food is both a tradition and a treat. It consists of things like black-eyed peas, chitterlings, hamhocks, pig's feet, pig's ears, collard greens, turnip greens, fried fish, fried chicken, sweet potatoes, candied yams, macaroni and cheese, corn bread, sweet potato pie, and sweet iced tea! Usually the things that taste the best to you aren't always the best for you. What a shame.

Jesus saw feeding the soul as more essential to survival than natural food. The soul food (hamhocks and chitterlings) that goes into the mouth and stomach of man passes through him because it is temporal and earthly (Matthew 15:17). On the other hand, the "soul food" that goes into the heart of man produces a bountiful harvest (Matthew 13:8,23). The Word of God does to the soul of man what food does to the body of man. Both bring life-giving nutrients that are essential for survival. And just as you get hungry, and satisfy the hunger by eating, so when your soul hungers and thirsts after righteousness, it ought to be filled. Our soul food is God's Word.

All that YOU SAY IS ALL that I need

To have a balanced diet means eating foods from the five basic food groups: breads and cereals, fruits and vegetables, meats and poultry, and dairy products. Just as we need this variety for health and survival, so we need the variety of things we receive from the Word of God.

Psalm 19:10 likens the Word of God to honey. Honey speaks of sweetness. The prophet Ezekiel said the Word entered his mouth and was very sweet (Ezekiel 3:3). There are times the Word of God is sweet to the taste and other times its contents can be bitter like castor oil (Revelation 10:10). There are some Sundays when your pastor will preach sweet "ice cream" sermons, while other Sundays he may preach "vegetable" sermons. Both deliveries are necessary for spiritual growth.

First Peter 2:2 likens the Word of God to pure milk. Just as babies need milk to survive and grow, Christians also need the Word of God to thrive spiritually. Can you imagine a newborn baby missing a day or two of feeding? That would be detrimental to its health, and probably fatal to its development. The same is true for a believer, especially a new believer. You can't afford to skip a day or two in the Word of God. The elementary principles of the faith cannot be obtained by osmosis. No matter how old we may get in the Lord, the sincere milk of the Bible is still vital and good for us. We can never hear the foundational principles of the Christian faith too often. The milk of the Word—it does the body good!

Hebrews 5:12-14 compares the Word of God to meat or solid food. The meat metaphor speaks of spiritual maturity. Spiritual maturity is being able to digest and apply biblical teaching. Regardless of how old we may be in the Lord, if we don't apply the Word of God consistently in our lives, we are still in spiritual diapers. Baby Christians may not know all of "Daddy's" teachings about the difference between good and evil (Hebrews 5:14), but mature Christians ought to know. Paul couldn't give the Corinthian church the meat of the Word because they acted like babies by whining and bickering with one another (1 Corinthians 3:1-3). This congregation should have been on a diet of solid food and able to feed others, but, in fact, they were still on the bottle.

Sometimes we can be more concerned about what we put into our bodies than what we put into our spirits. We faithfully read the nutrition information on the back of food items to make sure we aren't eating too many calories, carbohydrates, or sugars. This is a great discipline and shows good stewardship of our bodies. We must remember, however, that the outward man is still perishing and the inward man has to be renewed daily if we are to grow spiritually and be spiritually healthy (2 Corinthians 4:16). We need to be more diligent to read and apply the nutrition facts that are in the Word of God because we must remember, "We are what we eat."

A Word for Me

Proverbs 25:25

REV. CHRIS WILLIAMSON

There are some people whose favorite part of the day is the trip to the mailbox. Their hope is finding a letter there from a friend. The truth of the matter is that we all like receiving a personalized letter or a package from those we love. It lets us know that we were thought of and that someone took the time to bless us with a kind word. Proverbs 25:25 says, "Like cold water to a weary soul is good news from a distant land."

Personal letters to a missionary in the field are much more satisfying to their soul than an impersonal check for their banking account. An inmate who receives a personal letter from a family member or a friend is the envy of the cell block. A personal letter from a parent to a child in summer camp, or vice versa, is a delightful, tear-jerking gift. Letters like these have a tendency to arrive right on time. They often come just when we most need a word of encouragement. Yet if a letter from someone far away can bless us like this, how much more a timeless letter from the Almighty God who lives in the distant heavens?

The transcendent God, who created the universe by speaking the Word, wants to speak His Word into our lives and do some recreating in us! The infinite God, who measured the waters in the hollow of His hand, has a personal word for us! The lover of our soul wants to bless our soul with a personalized message! God's personal letter to us is contained in the Bible, and it is the best news one could ever receive. For in His letter to us we find His mind and will on all matters pertaining to life (2 Timothy 3:16,17).

Some Christians forfeit hearing from God through His Word because of the pressing business of life. "I don't have the time," we sometimes say when it comes to reading God's Word, but isn't it amazing how we make time for everything else like our favorite television show, novel, magazine, or newspaper? We all make time for who and what we deem as important.

Some Christians give up reading the Bible because it's too hard and nothing jumps off of the pages at them. But the Bible is such that the more we get into it, the more it gets into us. Proverbs 2:4,5 compares getting the wisdom of God to digging for treasure. No one hits paydirt or strikes oil with the first swing. We've got to be persistent and consistent. We must also read with the attitude of dependence upon God's Spirit to teach us (1 Corinthians 2:9-16). Consider a child's pop-up book: For the first couple of pages nothing may jump out at you, but keep turning the pages and it will! Then you'll find yourself unable to put it down.

Other Christians read the Bible without a plan, and they feel like it is incomprehensible. When looking for something to read, we shouldn't treat the Bible like a glorified roll-a-dex. "Eeni, meeni, mini, moe. . .where she stops nobody knows!" I heard a story about a man who would close his eyes, open his Bible, and let his finger randomly come to rest on a text of Scripture. Whatever he blindly pointed at, he would read and apply for that day. One day he read Proverbs 6:6 which says "Go to the ant. . ." so he started an ant farm. Another day he read Ecclesiastes 11:1 "Cast your bread upon the waters. . ." so he started feeding the ducks at the park. Then He read Matthew 6:6, which says, "Go into your room and close the door. . ." No one has seen him since 1975!

We cannot depend on our pastor alone for our intake of spiritual food from the Bible. God does gift certain people to teach His Word (Ephesians 4:11,12), but we'll starve and have no spiritual weight if we only eat on Sundays and Wednesday nights. God wants to teach us things that no man can teach us (1 John 2:27).

When the gas gauge in our car reads "empty," we know that we had better stop for a fill-up real soon. Only the filling station can provide what we need. We can't go to the grocery store for a fill-up. We can't go to the library for a fill-up. Only the gas station has the fuel we need for our cars to function. It is an unwise person whose car is on empty (usually hurrying and running late to make an appointment), but just drives on by the gas stations saying to themselves, "I can make it, I can make it!" Later, they will probably find themselves broken down on the side of the road. If only they had stopped and taken the time for a fill-up.

When our spiritual tanks are empty and we're riding on fumes, it's time to stop for a fill-up. Only God has what we need in order to be filled. His filling station is our prayer closet and His fuel for us is His Word. When we pass up spending time with Him, saying to ourselves, "I can make it, I can make it!" we'll soon find ourselves broken down on the side of the road of life, waiting desperately for a spiritual tow.

Speak while MY HEART is near

The Holy Spirit within us quickens our mortal bodies as we are fed the Word of God (Romans 8:11). Jesus said, "The Spirit gives life; the flesh counts for nothing. The words I have spoken to you are spirit and they are life" (John 6:63). The Greek word used for "life" is *zoe*, which means motion or activity. This is life that moves and grows. If you are finding that your spiritual tank is on E, you need to spend time in the Word of God, letting God communicate to your heart and mind from the message He has for you. To receive a personal letter from God, we don't have to wait for the mailman. All we need to do is open up the pages of God's Word.

The Whole Counsel of God

Acts 20:27

REV. CHRIS WILLIAMSON

he Church Hop is a new dance craze that is sweeping America. The Church Hop begins when a pastor steps on someone's toes in the congregation by preaching uncompromisingly from the Word of God. Perhaps it is a sermon about financial stewardship, marriage and divorce, submission, the gifts of the Spirit, or holy living. Whatever it is, the weight of the Word dropping into a life that doesn't want to hear it causes a person to grab their foot, jump up and down, and holler and complain while hopping out the door to another church. Hopefully, when they get to the next church the pastor won't step on that same problem area. If he does, the Church Hop begins again.

Pastors who teach the whole counsel of God's Word (Acts 20:27 NKJV) are not trying to step on toes for the sake of wounding people with the Bible. No, they are trying to be faithful to God and His Word, knowing that they are under stricter judgment concerning how they handle it (James 3:1). Expository teaching, like no other homiletical style of presenting the Word, causes the speaker and the listener to deal with the text as a whole from a historical, grammatical, contextual, and literary perspective. When reading the Bible we need to remember that it occurred in a different era, culture, and historical backdrop. Therefore, before we apply any given text to our modern experience, we should first seek to understand who wrote it, to whom it was written, how it was written, why it was written, and what impact it had on its initial hearers.

One of the signs of the end of the age is a lack of tolerance for sound, biblical teaching (2 Timothy 4:3,4). In fact, some people will go out of their way to find teachers who will tickle their ears, telling them just what they want to hear. But there is usually a great difference between what we want to hear and what we need to hear. What we need to hear has the capacity to change our lives, whereas what we want to hear may end up costing us our lives. Any doctor, lawyer, teacher, or pastor worth their salt will tell us what we need to hear, even if it's not what we want to hear. Then it's up to us to decide what we are going to do with the truth we have heard.

55

Second Chronicles 18 tells us how Ahab, the wicked king of Israel, asked Jehosaphat, the king of Judah, to join him in war against Ramoth Gilead. Jehosaphat said that he would help out on the condition that Ahab "first seek the counsel of the Lord." In other words: Going to war sounds like a good idea, but is it God's idea? We shouldn't make plans and then ask God to join us or bless us as an afterthought. No, we should seek out what His plans are, as recorded in His Word, and join Him!

Ahab had four hundred prophets on the payroll, who all told him what he wanted to hear: "Go to war, God will give you victory." But Jehosaphat knew that something was fishy, so he asked if there a true prophet in the house. The name Micaiah came up, and King Ahab immediately grabbed his toes and started doing the Church Hop. He said, "I hate him because he never prophesies anything good about me, but always bad" (2 Chronicles 18:7).

When Micaiah was summoned, he told Ahab what he didn't want to hear. He told him that defeat was inevitable. Micaiah didn't have time for ear tickling, nor was he trying to win a popularity contest with the king. He had a greater King in the heavens to answer to (2 Timothy 4:1,2). This prophetic counsel from God got Micaiah slapped and put into prison (2 Chronicles 18:23-26). John the Baptist later knew about this kind of persecution for not tickling the ears of a ruler. It got him a "Go to Jail" pass and his head on a platter (Matthew 14:3-11). Ahab disregarded the whole counsel from God and did his own thing. This ultimately cost him his life.

If we're going to be serious about the whole counsel of God's Word, we can't be only New Testament saints. That's like watching *Rocky III* and *IV* without watching *Rocky I* and *II!* You couldn't really appreciate or understand what's going on without the foundation being laid first. And what's with these "New Testament only" Bibles? You don't have half a road map, half a phone book, or half a cookbook. A doctor doesn't have half a medical book, nor a lawyer half a law book. Neither should a Christian, who has access to a whole copy of God's Word, have just half a Bible.

Christians shy away from the Old Testament for many poor reasons. When Paul said in 2 Corinthians 3:2,3 that we are to be "living epistles" (or walking Bibles), the New Testament was obviously not yet complete, for he was still writing it! When he told Timothy that all Scripture is God-breathed and profitable for doctrine, reproof, and instruction in righteous living so that the man of God might be thoroughly equipped to every good work (2 Timothy 3:16,17), all Timothy had access to was the Old Testament.

The ministry of Jesus was based on teaching from the Old Testament (Luke 4:16-21) and fulfilling it (Matthew 5:17). The preincarnate Jesus can even be found in the Old Testament on several occasions as the "Angel of the Lord" (Genesis 16:7, 22:15). You can even find Him if you look for Him behind the articles of the tabernacle, the symbolism of the feasts, and the significance of the sacrifices. The two covenants don't contradict, they complement. The Old Testament concealed is the New Testament revealed.

Finally, there are Christians who stay away from the book of Revelation because they say it's too complicated. But we need to consider the fact that God would never give us a book of the Bible that we couldn't understand. His Holy Spirit will teach us (John 14:26) and lead us into all truth, if we are willing to ask for His wisdom (1 Corinthians 2:9-13). In fact, the book of Revelation is the only book of the Bible that specifically promises a blessing to the reader (Revelation 1:3).

Next time you find yourself tempted to do the Church Hop, remember that it is our responsibility to take the whole of the Scriptures into account, not just the parts we happen to be comfortable with. The whole counsel of God is a gift given to help us grow. Let us look to it to help us live our lives in a way that pleases God.

Seven blesseds in the book of Revelation

1:3
14:13
16:15
19:9
20:6
22:7
22:14

The Flawless Word of God

Psalm 18:30

REV. CHRIS WILLIAMSON

Have you ever read a good book and then said to someone, "I just finished a gem last night?" When a book is called a gem that usually means it "brightened" up the life of the reader in one way or another. Our libraries, both public and personal, ought to be overflowing with precious gems. *Pilgrim's Progress* is a gem. *The Adventures of Huckleberry Finn* is a gem. *Romeo and Juliet* is a gem. *War and Peace* is a big gem!

Usually when we refer to a gem, we are talking about a rare precious stone. There's the onyx, jasper, ruby, emerald, and sapphire to name just a few. But the greatest of all gems is the diamond. Diamonds get their unlikely start as pieces of coal. But through time, heat, and the pressure of the earth, a piece of coal can be transformed into a glistening diamond, just as grains of sand become a pearl within an oyster.

The value of diamonds is contingent upon how flawless they are. Just because a diamond is very large may not mean that it is worth more than one that is smaller. The larger diamond may have flaws in it that causes its value to be diminished. Flaws in diamonds come in the form of abrasions, glitches, and scratches to the surface which arise from natural or accidental causes. These imperfections hinder light from traveling through the diamond effectively, not allowing it to reflect its natural brilliance and luster. And what value is a diamond that doesn't shine?

The classic books mentioned above (and others like them), are literary gems indeed, but they are not without flaws. They are flawed because a flawed, finite person wrote them. They show their limitations. They may be able to delight your soul, but they can't save it.

But when we discuss the Bible in relation to literary masterpieces, you're in an entirely different category. The Bible claims to be the Word of God over 600 times, and as such, the light of its Eternal Author permeates this completely unique book, producing a message and a power unlike any other.

Consider what the Bible says about itself:

> As for God, his way is perfect; the word of
> the LORD is flawless... (Psalm 18:30).

> And the words of the LORD are flawless,
> like silver refined in a furnace of clay, purified
> seven times (Psalm 12:6).
>
> Every word of God is flawless. . . (Proverbs
> 30:5).

The Hebrew word used in each of these verses means "to purge, purify, or refine by fire in order to separate the impurities." But I know what you may be thinking, "Didn't flawed men write the Bible, too? What makes it any different from other literary gems?"

For one thing, the Bible is inspired. No other book can make that claim. The writings of Homer or Shakespeare may be inspirational, but they are not inspired in the purest sense of the word. The Greek word for "inspired" literally means "God-breathed." The Scriptures of the Old and New Testament are God-breathed (2 Timothy 3:16; 2 Peter 3:15,16) in that God by His Spirit miraculously worked through men to produce His thoughts in a written form. These men that God used were called "holy men" (2 Peter 1:19-21 KJV). They ranged from prophets to kings, from generals to statesmen, even tax gatherers to doctors. They were normal people, supernaturally chosen and empowered by God to record His kingdom agenda and the panorama of redemptive history in their own literary style and historical setting. In the writing of the Bible, the Divine engaged with the human without the human element contaminating the content. The result is a book like no other, a flawless account of God's revelation to man.

A further reason we can trust that the Bible is flawless is its record of fulfilled prophecy (detailed predictions concerning the birth, life, death, and resurrection of the Messiah, the regathering of Israel, and other historical events), as well as its archeological confirmation (The Dead Sea Scrolls, for example). The fact that the text of the Bible was preserved intact through thousands of years is another earmark of its authenticity. Space does not allow us to even begin to touch upon all the evidence that points to a supernatural origin for the Bible. The fact that the Bible was written on three different continents (Asia, Africa, and Europe), over a 1,400 year period, by over 40 different authors yet still is uniform in its message, is certainly a miracle. The fingerprints of God are all over the Bible's unique character.

Flaws in a diamond usually cannot be detected with the naked eye. Unless you are a certified jeweler, you probably wouldn't know what to look for. But, with the aid of a monocle or a magnifying lens, you can discover the extent of the flaws. Ultimately, the price of the diamond is connected with its quality. The lower the price, the more flaws; the higher the price, the fewer the flaws.

For hundreds of years, cynics and skeptics have put the Bible under the lens of scrutiny in order to discover its flaws. Men have published theories, dissertations, and theses which attempt to undermine the foundations of Christianity. But time and time again, these intelligent searchers have come away from their examination shaking their heads, sometimes even converted, because the Word of the Lord ended up examining *them* (Hebrews 4:12). C.S. Lewis and Josh McDowell are perfect examples.

The most valuable diamond in the world is said to be the Hope Diamond. It is valued as priceless. Because of those who might steal it, it is constantly under guard. Many people will never see this diamond except in a picture. The privileged few who are able to see the Hope Diamond aren't able to hold it because of its incredible value. To actually own it would be out of the question even for the most financially affluent people in the world.

But there is a diamond, if you will, that is even more valuable than the Hope Diamond. This diamond offers *real hope* that transcends the temporal realities of this life and soars into the realm of eternal significance. The hope that this diamond contains can lift any head which hangs low, allowing *The Fingerprints OF GOD ARE ALL over the Bible* the King of Glory to come in (Psalm 24). This diamond is truly priceless, but nevertheless can be owned by anyone and everyone. This flawless gem masterfully comes from the heart of God and its worth is not based upon market value, size, cut, or man's opinion. Rather, its value is known by those who do not merely own it, but also treasure it. And the proof of whether or not we appreciate this treasure, is if we dig into it (Proverbs 2:1-5), seeking to glean from the sparkling wisdom of this inexhaustible gem we call the Bible.

BREATHE ON ME, BREATH OF GOD

Words by Edwin Hatch
Music by Robert Jackson
and Phil Naish

Breathe on me, Breath of God,
Fill me with life anew.
That I may love what Thou dost love,
And do what Thou wouldst do.

Breathe on me, Breath of God,
Until my heart is pure.
Until my will is one with Thine,
To do and to endure.

Breathe on me, breathe on me,
So that I will never die.
Breathe on me, breathe on me,
Grant me everlasting life.

Breathe on me, Breath of God,
Till I am wholly Thine.
Until this earthly part of me
Glows with Thy fire divine.
Until this earthly part of me
Glows with Thy fire divine.

Educated at Wheaton College, Northern Baptist Seminary, and Regent University, Tom Moucka is the founding pastor of Franklin Fellowship Church. This year he celebrates 21 years in the ministry, including nine years with Young Life. Tom believes in putting the gospel into action and is very involved in a number of community activities. The devotions Tom has written for this book wed the two aspects of his spiritual life: sound theology and vibrant personal faith.

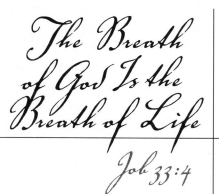

The Breath of God Is the Breath of Life

Job 33:4

TOM MOUCKA

When I was learning CPR in an Emergency Medical Technician course, I learned that the first priority for a stricken victim is to get his/her breath restored. It is essential to get them breathing again. You can artificially force the blood to circulate, but if that blood doesn't have oxygen in it, your efforts are in vain. In order for us to live and thrive we must be able to breathe, and if we cannot breathe for ourselves then we must get help from someone else. Sometimes I think our spiritual life is much like that. As Christians, who have the breath of new life within us, we often find ourselves stricken and in need of help from someone else. We need fresh breath blown into our spiritual lungs in order to revitalize our life with Christ. Only the Spirit of God can do that. It was Job who said, "The Spirit of God has made me; the breath of the Almighty gives me life" (Job 33:4). This is true not only for physical life, but for spiritual vitality as well.

It seems, however, that the daily demands of our occupations, families, friends, health, and just the routine upkeep in our lives are constantly threatening to squeeze the breath out of our life. We sometimes speak of living at "a breathless pace." But when we do, our spiritual life is the part of us that suffers most. When our daily schedule increases in complexity and something has to give, why is it that we open our calendars and cross out times of prayer, Bible Study, or worship? Why is it that we assume our spiritual life will somehow be unaffected by the low priority we give it? Is it that we know God will always be there anyway? Or is it that it's easy to hurt the ones you love? Or is it maybe just because we've grown so accustomed to spiritual mediocrity that we expect little out of our Christian experience? Whatever the cause, our need remains the same: the life-giving breath of God in our spirits.

The Good News is that God knows our needs and wants to meet them through His Son Jesus Christ. A few years ago, I was visiting the juvenile division of the Cook County Jail in Chicago. One of the volunteer chaplains, Gordon McClean, introduced me to a young man named Carlos. After some get-to-know-you chit-chat Gordon said to Carlos, "Tell Pastor Moucka why you're here." The young man looked me in the eye and said, "They say I shot a cop." Then the chaplain prompted him again, "What does that mean for you, Carlos?" Without flinching, his response was a clear and resolute, "I'll probably never get out of jail." I tried to share consoling and encouraging words with him, but he interrupted, saying, "Don't worry, pastor, I know Jesus. Compared to eternity, my time in here won't be long." I wondered if he could possibly know the full extent of that truth, so I asked him, "Carlos, the rest of your life is likely to be a very long time. Are you sure you're ready for that?" He smiled and said, "Pastor, you know what it's like to be with Jesus. These walls aren't big enough to contain Him!"

As I was leaving the detention center, working my way through the multi-layered security checkpoints, I found myself thinking of Carlos. He was right. Concrete walls and steel bars don't restrain Jesus. His love can fill the heart of a lost and lonely juvenile offender, His light can pierce the darkness of the darkest places, and His breath can breathe life into the most desperate of situations.

His light can pierce the darkness

Few of us are cop killers, and most of us will never spend a day of our lives in prison. But all of us can relate to an empty feeling inside or the temptation to fall into despair during the hard times. We can find ourselves questioning whether the grace of God really is sufficient for us.

Do we really believe that His power is made perfect in our weakness? (See 2 Corinthians 12:9.) For the patient in need of the life-giving breath of CPR the answer is, "Yes!" For Job in the midst of all his loss and pain, the answer is, "The breath of the Almighty gives me life!" For Carlos, living out his days in prison, the answer is, "Compared to eternity, my time in here won't be long." Yes, again and again, the answer is yes…for those who have stopped trusting their own ability to deliver them.

"Trust and obey, for there's no other way…" says the old hymn. The key to our deliverance is not to be found within ourselves, but in Christ, and Christ alone! His grace *is* sufficient, but only for those who avail themselves of it. If we stubbornly continue at a breathless pace trying to find fulfillment in advancement, acquisition, or acceptance, we will ultimately find ourselves in a cell too small for God. A cell created by our own self-reliance, a prisoner of no surrender. And here lies the irony. The only way to be set free is to confess. The only way to gain the victory is to surrender. The only way to receive the breath of life is to die.

Jesus taught us that "whoever wants to save his life will lose it, but whoever loses his life for me will find it" (Matthew 16:25). And, again, Jesus said, "I tell you the truth, unless a kernel of wheat falls to the ground and dies, it remains only a single seed. But if it dies, it produces many seeds. The man who loves his life will lose it, while the man who hates his life in this world will keep it for eternal life" (John 12:24,25).

These aren't politically correct ideas. You'll not find this taught in any of the popular psychological journals. Lose your life in order to save it? Hate your life to gain eternity? This message is foolishness to those who are perishing. But if we will only let go of the notion that our life is *our* life, if we will stop struggling as if our next breath depended on us, and if we will let God be God and breathe into us His breath of life, then we will surely live. Breathe on me, breath of God, fill me with life anew!

Thinking the Thoughts of God

Psalm 139:17

TOM MOUCKA

What would it be like to think the thoughts of God? Not only to know the truth, but also to be able to think the truth without interruption? Of course, outside of Christ, because of our sinful nature, this would be an alien experience to all of us. This dilemma is expressed in Isaiah 55:8,9:

> "For my thoughts are not your thoughts,
> neither are your ways my ways," declares the
> LORD. "As the heavens are higher than the earth,
> so are my ways higher than your ways and my
> thoughts than your thoughts."

The gulf between God and us impacts everything, even the way we think.

Before we can think the thoughts of God, we must deal with the separation caused by sin. Edwin Hatch, in his beautiful hymn, "Breathe On Me, Breath of God", seeks the breath of God to purify his heart "until my will is one with Thine." And so it must be. Our hearts need purifying and, because of sin, we cannot purify them ourselves. We need God, in His great mercy, to intervene and restore our fellowship with Him. That is exactly what He has done. Paul wrote to the Romans, "But God demonstrates his own love for us in this: While we were still sinners, Christ died for us" (Romans 5:8). The Good News is that, through the work of Jesus Christ, our sins can be forgiven and the separation caused by sin can be bridged. "But now in Christ Jesus you who once were far away have been brought near through the blood of Christ" (Ephesians 2:13). Many only think of these verses in terms of salvation. But this message is true not only for

"until my WILL IS ONE with Thine"

salvation, but also for our hope of increasing intimacy with the Father. As we daily bring our sins to the Lord and seek His purifying forgiveness, we can know oneness with Him. Again, we can see this in Paul's letter to the Corinthians, "But he who unites himself with the Lord is one with him in spirit" (1 Corinthians 6:17).

The key to thinking the thoughts of God is the Spirit of God. Paul says that no one knows the thoughts of God except the Spirit of God (1 Corinthians 2:11). That is what makes those who have been born of the Spirit different. As Christians, "we have the mind of Christ" (1 Corinthians 2:16).

The idea of having the mind of Christ really shouldn't be so hard for us to conceive of. After all, have you noticed how couples who have been married to one another for many years often finish each other's thoughts? The other day I was at a local bakery/restaurant and there was a sweet older couple just in front of me in line. As they were making their selection, their conversation went something like this:

"Oh, let me see…I…I know…I'd like…" the older gentleman pondered aloud. When he hesitated for just a moment, his wife finished his thought, saying, "…the almond turnover."

Obviously delighted, the man said, "Yes! Yes! That's just what I was thinking. Perfect. Now, how about you, dear?"

His diminutive wife, with her silver hair pulled back and a twinkle in her eye, said, "Oh, I just can't decide. It all looks so good. Hmmm, maybe…"

And with the pause, as if on cue, her husband said almost suggestively, "Maybe the pecan roll?"

With a satisfied smile and a confirming nod, she agreed. "Oh, I don't know why I hesitated. You know I love pecans." By the time I got to the counter I was grinning from ear to ear, bemused by the dear couple and delighted in their oneness. Oh, to be so united with Christ that we should hear Him as He completes our thoughts or—better yet—to hear the inner testimony of the Spirit and know its end.

But is it realistic to hope to think the thoughts of God? Is it even right to desire such a thing? Yes! Our God created us for intimate fellowship with Him. Jesus prayed that we would enjoy the same kind of intimacy as He enjoyed with the Father (John 17:22,23). Philippians 4:8 gives us some insight into how God thinks when Paul tells them what they should ponder: "Finally, brothers, whatever is true, whatever is noble, whatever is right, whatever is pure, whatever is lovely, whatever is admirable—if anything is excellent and praiseworthy—think about such things." Such characteristics arise out of the character of God Himself, they arise from within Him. As we think these kinds of thoughts we are thinking the thoughts of God.

Where do we find things that are true, noble, right, and so on? Sadly, they are hard to find these days. However, these godly thoughts come from God and we can find them where we learn of God...in His Word. Time in the Word of God is like time on the phone with a loved one.

Recently I was working on some continuing education with a seminary on the east coast. My days were spent in lengthy lectures and my evenings with intensive study at the library. When I finally arrived back at my room late at night, I was anxious to call home and talk to my wife. When I heard her voice on the other end of the phone, I could feel myself relax. We would chat about the children, the events of the day, the weather, whatever. It really didn't matter. We just enjoyed the time together. Our time on the phone was not as sweet as our weekly dates, but it was the next best thing until we were reunited at home. That's the way I feel about studying my Bible. It's not as good as face-to-face (that will have to wait until I get "home"), but it's the next best thing. In the Scriptures I can find the good things of God. Through them I can think the thoughts of God.

The writer of Proverbs reminds us that as a man thinks in his heart, so is he. The result of our time with God is the transformation of our hearts. As we think the thoughts of God our hearts become more and more like His, because the thoughts we are thinking come straight from His heart. Our whole person is changed into His likeness, bit by bit. Paul admonished the church in Rome, "...be transformed by the renewing of your mind" (Romans 12:2). It is God's intention that we be conformed to His likeness (Romans 8:29), so let us purpose to submit ourselves to the promptings of the Holy Spirit, dwell with God in His Word, and think His thoughts after Him. As we do this, we will find ourselves participating in the mind of Christ.

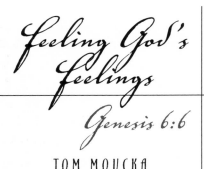

Feeling God's feelings

Genesis 6:6

TOM MOUCKA

When I was a new Christian, I was often told not to trust my emotions, but instead to trust God. I was taught that the Christian life was like the cars of a train. Faith is the engine, facts are the passenger cars, and feelings are the caboose. Feelings are fickle and undependable, God is not. Feelings change, God does not. Feelings are not real, but God is. The result of this kind of teaching was that feelings took a back seat, or like the great freight trains of today, the caboose was ultimately deemed unnecessary and left off altogether. I came to believe that emotions were, in fact, contrary to the ways of God. What never occurred to me then was that some of my emotions might be a reflection, though an imperfect one, of the heart of God Himself.

In our modern American culture, emotions are often looked upon as a sign of weakness. A person who is highly emotional is viewed as a person who is not entirely stable. A business associate too dependent upon his or her emotions is often seen as a liability in a business situation. And little boys who cry easily are labeled crybabies. Yet, at the same time there is a growing movement calling men to be more sensitive. In our new definition, a real man today is one who is "in touch with his feelings."

Not long ago I was at a fundraising dinner and the topic of conversation at our table was how much the roles for men and women have changed. In short order the men at the table began trying to "one up" each other to demonstrate how sensitive and thoroughly contemporary they each were. One man revealed he wasn't ashamed of crying while watching a movie. In fact, he informed us, he practically bawled at the end of a recent WWII movie. Another man said that he even cries while watching romantic comedies with his wife. And not to be outdone, still another confessed that he was dabbing his eyes at the conclusion of *The Little Mermaid*. Everyone was impressed at this great sensitivity and his vulnerability in sharing it. I must admit, though, that the whole scene reminded me of how little men have really changed after all. In typical male fashion, we were engaged in a very traditional,

we are made IN THE IMAGE *of God*

winner-takes-all competition over who was the most '90s-like sensitive man at the table! And besides. . . I like the *music* in *The Little Mermaid* too.

In reality, emotions are not a sign of weakness nor are they a badge of honor. Our feelings are just part of who we are, much like our five senses. God made us that way. And if that is true, then because we are made in the image of God, emotions are also a part of who God is. That's right. God has feelings too. Remember the episode in the Garden of Eden? God's creation was spoiled by mankind's self-centered rebellion. Soon the disease of sin had spread to the extent that little was left untouched by its effects. "The LORD saw how great man's wickedness on the earth had become, and that every inclination of the thoughts of his heart was only evil all the time" (Genesis 6:5). It is important to note God's response to this widespread wickedness. "The LORD was grieved that he had made man on the earth, and his heart was filled with pain" (verse 6). Grief and pain filled God's heart. But there's more: The Hebrew word translated here as "grieved" is *nacham,* which literally means "to breathe heavily" or "sigh in pain." And the Hebrew word for "pain" in this instance is *atsab* which is literally translated "to carve the heart." Apparently, when we allow sin to undermine our relationship with the Lord, we are stabbing Him in the heart and causing Him to hurt deep inside.

God has feelings. It is a sobering thought that our actions and attitudes stir up such strong emotions within Him. Some might say that this allusion in Scripture is simply an anthropomorphism, humanizing God to make a point. They argue that it is not fair to attribute to God traits that are so human. However, Jesus' parables confirm this understanding of God as one who feels strong emotions.

I have always been fascinated with the parable of the prodigal son. A more appropriate label for the story might be "the parable of the Father's heart" because this parable reveals the heart of the Heavenly Father like no other. As the story goes, a self-serving, adventure-seeking younger son obtains his inheritance from his father in advance. He heads off to a distant land and squanders the money in partying and self-indulgence. While he is away, we can presume his father was going about his usual business with one exception—he was preoccupied with something. Apparently the hearers of the parable are invited to imagine the son, after "coming to his senses," making his way down the road toward home. The father, in his deep longing for his wayward son, never gives up hope and, ". . .while he was still a long way off, his father saw him" (Luke 15:20). The father's heart for his prodigal son had never changed. His love for him was so all-engrossing that it constantly drew the father's gaze into the distance, watching for the return of his beloved child. His heart is further revealed in his reunion exclamation, "Quick! Bring the best robe and put it on him. Put a ring on his finger and sandals on his feet. Bring the fattened calf and kill it. Let's have a feast and celebrate. For this son of mine was dead and is alive again; he was lost and is found." Do you hear it—the wonderful heart of God for the lost? Can you feel the passion? Do you hear the compassion? Yes, God feels. His heart aches for the lost!

If God's heart is for the lost, what else is there that moves the heart of God? There are many other things in Scripture we could point to, but consider the following: the Father's heart for the poor and the Father's heart for the Church. The psalmist exclaims, "Who is like you, O LORD? You rescue the poor from those too strong for them, the poor and needy from those who rob them" (Psalm 35:10). Isaiah further expresses the Lord's heart for the poor in Isaiah 58, when he suggests that true fasting, true service to our Lord, is to do justice, feed the hungry, shelter the poor, clothe the naked, and provide for your own family. Truly, God's heart beats for the poor.

And God loves His Church. "For we are to God the aroma of Christ among those who are being saved and those who are perishing" (2 Corinthians 2:15). Jesus' tenderness toward us is expressed in His high priestly prayer as He prays, "Father, I want those you have given me to be with me where I am. . ." (John 17:24). Our God feels strongly for us. His love for us is so strong, so deep, so elemental to His being, that He was willing to give anything to save us . . . even His only Son. Oh, the pure, undefiled feeling of God!

To feel the feelings of God is to be passionate about the purposes of God. If the Father's heart breaks over the plight of the poor, then let us rise up as defenders of the poor! If the Father's heart is for the Church, then let us stop distrusting our brothers and sisters in other denominations and begin to pray for revival in the Church! With Edwin Hatch, let us sing, "Breathe on me, breath of God, till I am wholly Thine; until this earthly part of me glows with Thy fire divine."

More Than Mimicry

John 5:19

TOM MOUCKA

A heart wholly surrendered to the Lordship of Jesus Christ is a heart to do the will of God. Jesus' own desire was to do the will of His Father. He said, "I tell you the truth, the Son can do nothing by himself; he can do only what he sees his Father doing, because whatever the Father does the Son also does" (John 5:19). Spiritual maturity is more than just mimicking; it is a submission of the will. Intimacy with the Father increases in direct proportion to our obedience to His Word.

The Son of God did just what He saw His Father doing. I guess that is how I was as a kid. I was blessed with a wonderful father and loved to do the same things he did. I remember watching my dad hammering nails in our basement when I was still a child. I watched him carefully and then tried to do it like he did. When I got it right I felt like I was just like him. I felt close to him. I sensed his approval. It wasn't until years later that I realized I was simply mimicking.

As a teenager I had much more opportunity for self-governance. I had the choice between obedience to his will and disobedient self-determination. When I chose to disobey, my father's love never changed, but I felt his disapproval. However, when I chose to trust his loving guidance and conform to his will, then I not only sensed his approval, but I also sensed I was becoming more like him.

As a junior in high school I took a class in architectural drafting. Many times I had passed by the drafting classroom and admired the detailed drawings. When I found out they actually got to build a model of their dream vacation home, I was hooked. Besides, Dad was a mechanical engineer and I thought maybe I could use his drafting kit. One of the ongoing concerns of my dad was that I was a terrible procrastinator, especially when it came to school. I can still hear him saying, "See it through to completion, Tom. Good intentions are not enough." Well, drafting was no exception. I finished the drawings of my vacation home by the due date and what a home it was! Unfortunately, as big and beautiful as the house was on paper, when it came to actually building the model, I discovered that I had bitten off more than I could chew. Many times my dad would ask me at the dinner table, "How's your building project coming, Tom?" To which I always responded with some sort of evasive answer like, "Oh, one thing's for sure, when it's finished it'll be a showpiece!" He'd look at me out of the corner of his eye and say, "Don't put it off too long or you'll be too far behind to catch up and still do a good job." "Don't worry, Dad, it's coming along just fine. It'll be okay. Really." I'd cheerfully assure him.

The truth was I was just barely finished with the foundation and had only a couple weeks left to complete it. Inside I was worried that once again I'd disappoint him. He loved me so much and was always encouraging me. But I just couldn't seem to get motivated.

One night after dinner, Dad said, "Tom, let's go down to the basement and cut some 2x4s." I wasn't sure what he was talking about, but when we got down there he pulled a big stack of balsa wood out of a sack and said, "You think this'll be enough?" I couldn't believe it—he had me figured out! Here he was, setting aside a night to help me get caught up. That night we cut reams of floorboards, stacks of 2x6s, piles of 4x4s and more 2x4s than I could have imagined. Our workshop looked like a miniature lumberyard! The next day I sheepishly brought home my foundation and we began gluing the model of my dream home together. After several evenings of work the lumberyard was gone and the house had taken its place. It looked awesome!

On the last day of class, just in the nick of time, I paraded in with my house hoisted upon my shoulder. Needless to say, I got an "A" for the project. Well, maybe I should say my dad and I got an "A." I was so pleased. In my family, all boys, expressions of affection were, shall we say, understated. But I felt I had to express my deep appreciation to my dad, so I wrote him a note. I told him how much I appreciated all his help. I told him how grateful I was for his encouragement. I told him I loved him.

Less than a month later my dad died of a sudden heart attack. It was hard—he was very special to me. In an effort to lessen the grief of my mom I decided to make the ultimate teen sacrifice—I cleaned up my room! When I finally cleared away the mess on top of my chest of drawers, there it was…my undelivered note to my dad. Good intentions had not been enough.

It was a hard lesson to learn and I'm still working on it. If we want to grow as persons we must tame our wills and bring them into submission to those God has placed in authority over us. And if we hope to grow spiritually we need to submit our wills to the will of God. Spiritual maturity is more than just mimicking; simply going through the motions is the height of religiosity. To be mature in Christ is a matter of the heart and the will, and it is surrender to the Lordship of Jesus Christ.

"Them that HONOR ME I will honor"

When I think of surrender, I think of Eric Liddell, whose story is told in the movie *Chariots of Fire*. In 1924, at the Paris Olympics, this young Scotsman shocked the athletic world by disqualifying himself from the 100-meters race because his Christian conviction would not permit him to run a preliminary heat on Sunday. After some consideration, Eric Liddell was instead entered in the 400 meters, for which he not only won the gold medal, but also set a new world record.

It is no wonder he is remembered as "Scotland's greatest athlete." But which came first, Eric Liddell's notoriety or his submission to God's authority? Liddell was a man of conviction—he had decided that honoring God was more important than the personal honor and fame of Olympic glory. Interestingly, just before the 400-meters race a note was slipped into Liddell's hand. It was a passage of Scripture, 1 Samuel 2:30: "Them that honor me I will honor."

But I think he knew this even before he received the note. He did what he did without any guarantee in the 400 meters. He did what he did because he trusted God more than the accolades of man. He did what he did because he understood the correlation between intimacy with God and obedience. Intimacy with the Father increases in direct proportion to our obedience to His Word.

If I had listened to my father's loving advice I might have been spared some difficult times later on in school. Moreover, if I had obeyed his admonitions I would have communicated my deep love for him. Still, the incredible thing is that if we will obey our Heavenly Father—love what He loves and do what He does—we will grow in spiritual maturity and spend an eternity in deeper and deeper communion with Him. And one day I'll get my chance to say to my earthly father in heaven, "I love you, Dad."

HE IS GOOD

*Words and Music
by Frank Hernandez*

He is good, He is good
His love endures forever,
Give thanks to the Lord, for He is good.
He is good, He is good,
His love endures forever,
Give thanks, for He is good.

He is good, He is good
His love endures forever,
Give thanks to the Lord, for He is good.
He is good, He is good,
His love endures forever,
Give thanks, for He is good.

For His unfailing love
And His wonderful deeds,
Give thanks, give thanks to the Lord.

He is good, He is good
His love endures forever,
Give thanks for He is good.

For His unfailing love
And His wonderful deeds,
Give thanks, give thanks to the Lord.

He is good, He is good
His love endures forever,
Give thanks to the Lord, for He is good.
He is good, He is good,
His love endures forever,
Give thanks, for He is good.
Give thanks, for He is good.

Denny Denson grew up on the streets of inner-city Chicago, where he first experienced the grace and love of God. A graduate of Moody Bible Institute and Chicago Baptist Institute, Denny is the pastor of First Missionary Baptist Church in Franklin, Tennessee. He is active in his community, working with programs for the under-privileged as well as outreach to gangs and drug abusers. The themes that run through all Denny's devotions are the goodness and faithfulness of God. For him, these truths are not abstract theological concepts, but are based on his own experiences with God.

Unfailing Love

Psalm 107:1

DENNY DENSON

hen we sin, we are sometimes so over-come by guilt that we begin to wonder if God is through with us, that we have messed up just one too many times. We fear His anger and wrath against us. But the amazing thing that happens is that God meets us with love rather than condemnation. Instead of receiving wrath, the repentant man or woman receives grace, mercy, and forgiveness. Instead of God's disfavor with us, we experience His unfailing love.

To truly understand the depth of God's love, we have to know His heart towards us. This is not something we can come to know in our own strength. In fact, it goes against our usual way of thinking to believe that God could really love us as much as He does. We can only understand God's love because it has been extended to us. In Christ, God reached out toward us. Through Him, we come to understand God's long-suffering, His patience, and His compassion toward us.

We do not deserve the kind of love God gives. But still, God does not give up on us. In the very beginning, mankind was created perfect: holy and upright, without blemish. But man sinned and rebelled against God's love, falling from the place of perfection. We decided to go our own way and left the path God intended for us. But He found the way for His love to endure. He found the path that would bring us back to Him. He is still in the business of doing that today for those who are His children.

In Christ, GOD REACHED OUT toward us

The story of David provides us with a perfect example of God's unfailing love. He was the great king of Israel, and God had blessed him richly with gifts and talents. He was even called "a man after God's own heart." But what did he do with the love and responsibility that God had given him? He used it to follow his own fleshy desires. He committed unspeakable acts of disobedience. And yet, despite all that David did, God still loved him. Though he had been guilty of murder, adultery, and deceit, God did not give up on him. He forgave Him. If that is the case, why would we ever think He would give up on us?

Or think of Peter, the apostle. Jesus said that He would build His church on Peter's confession of faith. Yet Peter denied Jesus. Did God give up on him? No. Even the best of our friends or family members would eventually run out of patience with us if we acted as David or Peter had. But not God.

Sometimes we have to be pretty hard on our own children. We find ourselves having to say things like, "This is the last time. I can't overlook this kind of behavior anymore." And we will often let the penalty fall on our children, no matter how much they beg and plead. But not God. He may allow us to suffer the consequences of our actions, but He will always be there to redeem the situation. He will not allow us to perish.

I know the truth of God's unfailing love from my own life. I was one who challenged His reality and denied His existence. I *was* the prodigal son. But even after all the times I failed Him or was disobedient to His ways, still His love did not turn away from me. Like the father in the parable of the prodigal son, God patiently waited for me to return and when I did He received me with open arms. He did not shut me out while I was rebellious against Him. He continued to love me.

But God's love is such that He doesn't just want to be there to pick us up when we fall. He wants to walk intimately with us, showing us the path we should follow. He wants to be our life manager. It's not enough just to know God intellectually or emotionally. The question we must continually ask ourselves is: "Is God my life manager? Do I allow Him to manage my life?" To use the language of the Bible, we must ask ourselves whether He is our *Lord*. Our life is His property. He owns us and we owe all to Him. Therefore, He must be in complete control. Only then will we experience the fullness of God's love.

We can never fully appreciate the love of God unless we experience it from the inside by letting Him change our hearts. If you don't know very much about art, you'll never appreciate a painting by Picasso or VanGogh. An art appreciation class would help you to see the finer points of their work and appreciate it more fully by being exposed to it like you never have before. It is only when you are exposed to the finer things in life that you really learn to appreciate them. It is the same with the love of God. We must experience it ourselves if we are to really appreciate it. We must expose ourselves to Him. We must become vulnerable to God. We must allow ourselves to be known by Him.

When a young man first meets a young lady, he is usually kind of reserved and so he holds part of himself back. He tells her that he is interested in her and attracted to her, but he doesn't reveal too much of himself. But as the relationship goes on, he lets more and more of himself be known by her. And the more he reveals, the more she determines that "Hey, I really like this guy!" Out of self-revelation, true love is born. It is the same with the love of God. He will not force Himself upon us. We must be brave enough to open ourselves up to Him. When we do, we will know His unfailing love.

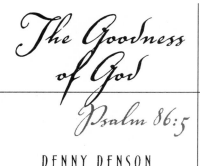

The Goodness of God
Psalm 86:5

DENNY DENSON

hy does God love us so much? Why is He so quick to forgive us? This is one of the great mysteries to us. Because we are not really good ourselves, it is hard for us to understand God's goodness. But goodness is in God's very nature. It is part of His essence. In a certain sense, God can't help but be good. That is just who He is. God's goodness doesn't mean that we will always get what we want from Him. Nor does it mean that He will not chastise us at times for our sinful ways. But because He is good, He will not stop loving us. Ever.

Of course, God wants us to reflect some of His goodness. We can make the mistake of thinking that we are doing God a favor when we do good. We hope that He will notice and approve. But God is not impressed with all our religious "do-gooding." It is His love that allows Him to continue to work with us, not any good that we have done. We really can't do God any favors. All the favor really comes from Him!

We have nothing to offer God. Even when we offer ourselves, all we are offering Him is a wretch who has been undone by sin. We have nothing to bring to Him. Anything we bring He must redo and remake. He has to give us new life. He has to give us a new heart. He has to give us new desires and determinations.

He takes our nothing and makes something out of it. Even with our most sincere praise and love and worship, we cannot begin to give what is due to Him. And yet, He continues to bless us, to love us, to show us His goodness. He continues to spare our lives.

Sometimes we make the mistake of thinking that God loves us only when we repent of our sins and become His children. But we forget that God loved us even when we were against Him, even when we did not really know who He was. The Bible says, "While we were yet sinners, Christ died for us" (Romans 5:8). He was my Creator and He gave His Son for my life. He did this for me because that is His nature and character. He is good.

His goodness can also be experienced by His protection and grace, which comes to us in all kinds of ways that we don't expect. As one who grew up on the streets, I was involved in lots of situations I shouldn't have been able to walk away from unharmed. I look back now at the things I was involved in. Others who did the same things paid an awful penalty, some are now long gone from this world. But I was spared. God saw me through those times of trouble. We can make the mistake of thinking that we're awfully slick and smart enough to stay out of trouble. But we're not. It is only the hand of God that rescues and protects us. And as the Scripture says, "And we know that in all things God works for the good of those who love him, who have been called according to his purpose" (Romans 8:28). There is nothing we can go through that is larger than God's peace. God never promised that we wouldn't go through trials and tribulations, but He did promise that He would not leave us or forsake us.

The goodness of God is such that it even allows us to be mad at Him. Like David, we can yell and make a fuss and cry out that we don't understand. He loves us enough to make room for these kinds of feelings. Each of us is a unique creation, and God understands what "makes us tick." He isn't threatened if we argue with Him or complain that we are confused. Life is like a jigsaw puzzle. Every piece is part of God's plan. Nothing is accidental or incidental. When things happen that are not to our liking, we need to ask ourselves what it is that God wants to accomplish for our life from this experience. Because of His goodness, we know He will see us through.

The Peace of His Presence

Philippians 4:7

DENNY DENSON

God's presence has been with me throughout my life, sometimes when I didn't even realize it! I went to church as a child for one reason: because my mother wanted me there. I certainly wasn't interested! God didn't seem very real to me. But my mother was a praying woman, and she constantly held me up in prayer. Even when I rebelled against God and the church, she was faithful to pray for me. Even when my actions caused her a great deal of pain, she continued to lift me up before God, asking that He would make Himself real to me. God answered that prayer and continues to answer it today. Are there people who might be praying for the same thing for you?

The very first time I remember feeling the presence of God was when I was 19. At that age I was a very rambunctious and rebellious young man. One day I was staying at my uncle's house and was stretched out on the bed in the back bedroom, just lying there relaxing in the afternoon sun. Suddenly, I heard a voice. I thought it was my uncle calling me, so I got up and went into the front room. "Uncle, did you call me?" I asked.

"No," he answered, so I went back to the bedroom and lay back down.

Just as I was about to doze off, I thought I heard him call again. *I wonder what he's up to?* I thought to myself, but I went back out to the front room anyway. "No," he said, "I didn't call you."

When it happened a third time, I called to mind what my uncle had said to do if I heard the voice again. "The next time you think I call you," he had said, "just answer." And I did. Then the presence of God became so real to me that I became frightened, so I climbed off of the bed and went out to the front porch. At this point in my life, I had never heard the story of how God called Samuel, but when I later read about Samuel's call it reminded me a little of my own experience. God was answering my mother's prayer.

I had another unusual experience of God's presence a few years later. I was just sitting all by myself when a full-fledged sermon popped into my head. I'd never considered myself a candidate for the ministry, but if I'd been in church that day I could have preached a powerful message! I was overwhelmed that God would make Himself known in this way.

Of course, these are kind of unusual experiences. Like me, you've probably had a few unusual encounters with God.

But as I've grown in my relationship with Him, I've learned to sense the presence of God in a simpler, but no less profound way. He makes His presence known to me through bringing me His peace, and I've learned to be aware of His presence to the extent that I can be comfortable in any situation. The reason I can feel this way is that I know I'm never alone. His presence brings me peace. This peace is not just something I feel. It's something I know. I am never alone. Never. In the most troubling of times I can speak to God and He hears me. He is with me. Remember the promise Jesus made: "I am with you always" (Matthew 28:20). When we allow ourselves to gripe about life it is because we have forgotten the presence of God. The closer I get to God, the less I let things bother me. Awareness of God's presence grows as our intimacy with Him grows. We learn to sense Him because we know Him better. The presence of God is always there. He's been there all the time. The issue is not whether He's aware of me—He always is—but whether I'm aware of Him. We must decide whether we live in this awareness of His presence or shut Him out of our lives. But remember, when you shut off God, its like not paying your power bill. You are going to be in the dark!

I've learned to be aware of His presence

The presence of God brings peace to our hearts. I love what Jesus says in John 14:27: "Peace I leave with you; my peace I give you. I do not give to you as the world gives. Do not let your hearts be troubled and do not be afraid." That is probably my favorite promise in Scripture! Or I think of Philippians 4:7, which says, "And the peace of God, which transcends all understanding, will guard your hearts and your minds in Christ Jesus." God wants us to stay focused on Him. When we do, we will find the kind of peace that comes from knowing His reality and His precious presence with us.

Real Life
Psalm 112:1

DENNY DENSON

e are the recipients of so many bless-ings. Ultimately, the greatest of all blessings is the life that God gives to us. I am not referring to physical life, but to spiritual life. Without God, you cannot have this kind of life. And until He breathes His life into us, we aren't really even living.

When one doesn't really know God, all the things that he or she thinks are important are really just superficial. I know this from experience. I spent too many years out on the streets trying to impress people and playing the game. I came to learn that all the things I thought were pretty important really weren't important at all. I'm not just talking about material objects either. I found that people I thought were friends really were not. In this world, everybody is trying to outdo everybody else, always trying to figure out how to get an advantage. And success is not really success. There is no substance behind it. There is nothing to grasp hold of or hold onto when you really need help.

When you finally come to realize that *God is life*, things start to change. Everything becomes real. All things become important. Suddenly, everything matters. You get a new perspective. You get real life. Real life is when you can come home at night and praise God for the day He gave you and for the way He has been with you. You can lie down at night thanking Him for the day. And you don't dream bad dreams the way you used to.

Real life comes from God. Without God, our life just isn't quite real. A man can dig up his lawn and put in astroturf. It looks good, it has the advantage of being green year 'round, but it still isn't real. If you are a neighbor on the other side of the fence, you might say to yourself, "Boy, my neighbor's grass sure does look good!" But once you take a closer look, you realize it is fake! It just isn't the same as real grass. If you are looking for a nice lawn, this isn't the way to get it. Ultimately, it will not satisfy. It's the same thing with trying to live our lives without God. Without God we can only see the things that don't matter: nice cars, big houses, enviable power, or a good position in society.

Jesus said, "I have come that they may have life, and have it to the full" (John 10:10). This life is the essence of what our existence is meant to be. It's more than just breathing and eating. It is being alive in God.

One of the reasons that people aren't attracted to the gospel, why they don't throw themselves down at the feet of God, is because we who are His ambassadors don't look or act like we're really alive. We are often the only Bible this calloused world can read, and our type is crooked and our letters faint! Our message isn't very appealing because we don't look like we are truly alive. We should live in such a way that God's light shines through our lives. John 1:4 says of Jesus, "In him was life, and that life was the light of men."

His life arises out of His love. If we have His love, it should pour forth out of our lives. Jesus said, "A new commandment I give you: Love one another. As I have loved you, so you must love one another" (John 13:34). That is what people who don't know God are looking for: a true demonstration of God's amazing love. Jesus isn't impressed with us because we flow into the church on Sunday mornings or preach dynamic sermons or are a member of the choir or do a lot of missions work. He wants us to love one another. That is the way His life is shared.

Sometimes we take the life God gives us for granted. When we have His life within us, we become mindful of all the blessings He brings into our lives. We are reminded that all the good things in our lives ultimately come from Him. Flowing from His life within us are so many blessings, both great and small.

Several times in the Psalms, David prays, "Bless the Lord, O my soul." It is almost as if he is giving a pep talk to his soul, reminding it of its duty to bless God for the abundant life He has given. So, by the same token, should we stir up our souls to remember God's blessings and offer Him praise from our hearts. Everything in life can be a blessing because God is always reaching out to us. He continues to pursue us, desiring to shower us with His love and impart to us His life. Real life.

DOXOLOGY

Words by Thomas Ken

Music by Phil Naish

*A*wake my soul, and with the sun
Thy daily stage of duty run;
Shake off sloth, and joyful rise
To pay thy morning sacrifice.

Wake and lift up thyself, my heart,
And with the angels bear thy part,
Who all night long unwearied sing
High praise to the eternal King.

Praise God, praise God,
All creatures here below.
Praise God, praise God,
From whom all blessings flow.

Direct, control, suggest this day,
All I do, design, or say;
That all my powers, with all their might,
In Thy glory may unite.

Praise God, praise God,
All creatures here below.
Praise God, praise God,
From whom all blessings flow.

Praise the Father, praise the Son,
Praise the Spirit, Three in One.

Praise God, praise God,
All creatures here below.
Praise God, praise God,
From whom all blessings flow.

Praise God, praise God,
All creatures here below.
Praise God, praise God,
From whom all blessings flow.
From whom all blessings flow.

Mike Smith is an associate pastor at Christ Community Church in Franklin, Tennessee, and the author of Getting Ready for a Lifetime of Love. *As you'll see in his devotions, Mike has thought deeply and carefully about the place of worship in the life of the believer and has put these thoughts into practice in his own life.*

Understanding Leads to Praise

Luke 13:1-5

REV. C. MICHAEL (MIKE) SMITH

ood theology leads to doxology. When we think properly about the things of God (theology), it should lift our hearts in praise (doxology). Theology is the study of God, and doxology is a hymn of praise to God. The more you grow in understanding of the nature of God and His works the more your understanding will inspire and even demand praise. Praise comes forth spontaneously when God's works are made known through His redemptive history, and when those who delight in God contemplate His great actions we cannot but find worship within our hearts.

One of the most famous doxologies comes to us from the host of heavenly angels on the heels of the announcement made to the shepherds concerning the birth of Jesus. Luke records it for us in his Gospel account:

> An angel of the Lord appeared to them, and the glory of the Lord shone around them, and they were terrified. But the angel said to them, "Do not be afraid. I bring you good news of great joy that will be for all the people. Today in the town of David a Savior has been born to you; he is Christ the Lord" (Luke 2:9-11).

It was after this announcement that spontaneous praise erupted:

> Suddenly a great company of the heavenly host appeared with the angel, praising God saying, "'Glory to God in the highest, and on earth peace to men on whom his favor rests'" (Luke 2:13,14).

"Gloria in excelsis Deo" is Latin for "Glory to God in the highest," which is the chorus of the famous Christmas hymn "Angels We Have Heard on High." It was written to inspire us to carry on the celebration begun by the angels. It seems that the heavenly host could not contain their excitement and so praises rose to God as they contemplated the magnitude of what God had done in sending the Lord Jesus. They could not stand back and be spectators for this announcement. I enjoy imagining what it must have been like for those shepherds who were greeted by a heavenly chorus on that first Christmas. I imagine that the glorious music was probably accompanied by some sort of light show that filled the sky with spectacular celebration!

If a proper understanding of God and His works leads to praise, then it also true that misunderstanding of God and His works will lead to confusion and a heart that is hardened toward God. If biblical theology leads to great praise, then unbiblical theology will lead to great confusion about God. One of the things Jesus did in His ministry was to clarify common misunderstandings about the character of God the Father. One such occasion is recorded for us by Luke:

> Now there were some present at that time who told Jesus about the Galileans whose blood Pilate had mixed with their sacrifices. Jesus answered, "Do you think that these Galileans were worse sinners than all the other Galileans because they suffered this way? I tell you, no! But unless you repent, you too will all perish. Or those eighteen who died when the tower of Siloam fell on them— do you think they were more guilty than all the others living in Jerusalem? I tell you, no! But unless you repent, you too will perish" (Luke 13:1-5).

Can you see the common misunderstanding about God in relation to human tragedy that is reflected in the question Jesus is asked? The unspoken misconception behind the question was that those who suffered were being singled out and punished for some specific sin. Even today, some look at tragedies which occur and conclude that God must not be good, He doesn't care, or He is impotent to do anything about it. Failing to understand God properly leads to a misunderstanding of the meaning of human tragedy. Jesus responds to their question with one of His own which exposes the reality that they were asking the wrong question and thus coming to seriously wrong conclusions about God!

Jesus asks a revealing question, "Do you think they were more guilty than all the others living in Jerusalem?" He is letting them know that the question they should be asking is: "Why doesn't a tower fall on me?" or "Why was anyone spared at all?" In other words, why does God continue to tolerate our sin and rebellion against Him? Nobody at all really *deserves* to be spared from His wrath. Because God is so gracious and does not treat us as our sins deserve, we are sometimes lulled into complacency and take His kindness and mercy for granted. God does not owe His creatures anything! It is we ourselves (and Satan) who are responsible for sin and rebellion against God entering the world. Yet God is often given the blame for the tragedies which are caused by this rebellion. If we really understood our theology properly, we would understand that God is the One who works in redemptive history on behalf of His people. He has done something about Satan, sin, and death. It is by His grace and mercy that we have life and breath. It is by His grace and mercy that we have any ability to think and comprehend and care for others. It is when we take God's kindness, mercy, and grace for granted

Remember HIS RADICAL DISPLAY *of costly love*

that we are in danger of becoming confused about His nature, power, and compassion!

If you are ever in doubt that God really cares about His creation even as we were running from Him, remember His radical display of costly love demonstrated in the incarnation, cross, and resurrection of the Lord Jesus. Let me encourage you to contemplate the great themes of redemptive history. If you do, you'll surely break forth in spontaneous praise to the God who has acted on our behalf and come to our rescue! Write and sing your own doxology!

Begin with the incarnation. Jesus did not give up His deity at His human birth. He added to His divine nature a human nature so He could be the obedient Son and bring salvation to those who would believe in Him. Consider the atoning work of Christ Jesus at the cross and in His resurrection. Jesus has intervened on behalf of the people of God by drinking the cup of God's wrath to its very dregs! Then He conquered death by His resurrection. Then remember how the Lord gave us the Holy Spirit, securing our adoption into the family of God if we place our faith in Jesus. Finally, consider the consummation of all human history, when Christ will come again, bringing redemption to completion for His children!

When we understand what God has done for us it leads to praise. The apostle Paul understood this truth and knew how to ask the right question, "He who did not spare his own Son, but gave him up for us all—how will he not also, along with him, graciously give us all things?" (Romans 8:32). "Praise God from whom all blessings flow!"

A Heart for Praise

Psalm 33:1

REV. C. MICHAEL (MIKE) SMITH

As I grow in my Christian life, one of the things that becomes increasingly important to me is to develop a real heart of praise, where praise does not merely come from my lips, but arises out of the deepest levels of my heart. How is it that you and I can truly become people of praise?

I have found that you can use a variety of strategies to impact people's outward behavior, but you cannot really change their heart. Changing hearts is the work of God alone! This came home to me when my wife, Rinda, and I had our second child, Joel. I wanted to encourage our oldest son, Jimmy, to be kind and loving to his younger brother. You see, I had an older brother who would pick on and even torment me at times when we were children, and I wanted to protect Joel from some of the abuses I had experienced at his hands. My desire was that Jimmy would develop a true heart of love for his younger brother. But it did not take me very long to discover that no matter how hard I tried or how much I wanted it, I could not give Jimmy an attitude of love for Joel!

There were things I could do. I could be a model for him of what love toward his little brother would look like. I could instruct him about appropriate behavior and affirm good behavior while I discouraged that which was inappropriate. But, ultimately, I could not give my son a heart to love his younger brother. Only God could do that. When I thought about it, I realized that I could not even change my own heart. Changing my heart is the work of the Holy Spirit in my life. For my part, all I could really do was create an atmosphere in my life wherein I gave God more immediate access to my heart.

What does it mean to develop a heart of praise? I believe it means that we create an environment in our lives which allows the right kind of attitudes to grow and flourish in our hearts. It is similar to the process Paul points to in his first letter to the Corinthians: "I planted the seed, Apollos watered it, but God made it grow" (1 Corinthians 3:6). We can do the work of planting and watering to help create the environment for a heart of praise, but only God can make it grow!

We are sons and daughters of Adam and Eve. Eve's rebellion came in the form of doubting that God was good, that He cared for His creation, and that He had our best interests in mind. Adam's rebellion, on the other hand, was that he pridefully refused to submit to God. These two sins, unbelief

and pride, are at the core of our own rebellion against our
Creator God. If we are going to develop a heart of praise we
need to come to terms with our unbelief and pride.

Concerning unbelief, Jesus said that God requires us to
"believe in the one he has sent" (John 6:29). Since unbelief is
at the core of our rebellion against God, movement toward
Him requires believing Him and the one He sent, namely
Jesus. Regarding pride, the apostle Paul tells us this:

> For since the creation of the world God's invisible
> qualities—his eternal power and divine nature—
> have been clearly seen, being understood from
> what has been made, so that men are without
> excuse. For although they knew God, they neither
> glorified him as God nor gave thanks to him, but
> their thinking became futile and their foolish
> hearts were darkened (Romans 1:20,21).

Pride is failure to acknowledge our dependence on God
and render proper thanks to Him. For our hearts to move
toward God requires acknowledging our utter dependence
upon Him and offering thanks unto Him. Thus, developing a
heart for praise begins with acknowledging God, glorifying
Him, and giving thanks to Him. These are the first steps we
must make to create the environment in which a heart of
praise can grow.

Acknowledging God means turning from an attitude of
wanting to be independent of God to admitting our utter
dependence upon Him for both physical and spiritual life.
God does not owe His creation anything. He creates, reveals
himself to His creation, and restores fallen creatures at His

own discretion. He is the potter and we are the clay. We must admit that. It is something in which we can rejoice! Rejoice that He has seen fit to create us and has given us breath to praise Him. Rejoice that He sent His Son and that we can accept His atoning sacrifice, turning from our own attempts at making ourselves acceptable, depending entirely on Him.

Glorifying God means declaring His goodness and greatness. We do not give Him glory in the sense that He is lacking it without our words. Instead, we ascribe to the Lord the glory due Him. We tell of His wonders, sing of His grace, and shout of His greatness. We marvel at His love displayed to us through His Son, the Lord Jesus. As John Piper has said, is most glorified by us when we are most satisfied in Him." Finding our satisfaction in God alone brings Him glory and delight. He is the fountain of life, the source of living water! Finding satisfaction in lesser things robs God of the glory due Him. Therefore, find your fulfillment in Him, abandoning the lesser things that tend to obscure our need for God and God alone.

Giving thanks to the Lord God means declaring His labors on our behalf and owning up to our true status as creatures, not creators. Giving thanks shows our dependence on Him and strangles our prideful independence. This makes me think of Jack Miller's variation on the four spiritual laws: "Law one—God is God; Law two—You are not God; Law three—You confuse law one with law two; Law four—Get it straight!" When we praise and thank God, we are "getting it straight." We are humbling ourselves before Him. When we bend our knee and bow our head to Him we are acknowledging His sovereign rule over us and owning up to our desperate need for Him.

Praising God has much to do with offering God open access to our hearts. Of course, God doesn't need our permission to gain access to our hearts. At the same time, if we really want to develop a heart for praise, we can place our hearts and minds before Him and invite Him to change them. So set your minds and hearts on things above and give your praise to the Lord. "Praise Him all creatures here below!"

The Paradox of Praise

Matthew 6:33

REV. C. MICHAEL (MIKE) SMITH

Someone has referred to the Kingdom of God as "the upside down Kingdom." The standards of God's kingdom are very different from normal human expectations and are often the very opposite of what seems natural to us. In fact, God's truth can sometimes seem impossible for us to comprehend and contradictory to human reason. Yet it is true. We often refer to such truths as "paradoxes," and the Bible is full of them. The first shall be last and the last shall be first (Matthew 19:30). Whoever wants to be greatest must be the servant and whoever wants to be first must be slave of all (Mark 10:42-45). Hatred is conquered through love (Matthew 5:43-45). Or think of Jesus' call to discipleship, "For whoever wants to save his [or her] life will lose it, but whoever loses his [or her] life for me will find it" (Matthew 16:25). The ultimate paradox is that Jesus, the author of life, dies and gives life through His conquest of death (Acts 3:15; 2 Timothy 1:10).

The paradox presented to us by praise is that the obligation we have to praise our Creator actually liberates us. We rarely think of an obligation as something which leads to liberation. Instead, we tend to think that liberation comes when we are released from obligation. We want to be set free from our responsibilities to our Creator. Yet our Creator (who knows us all too well) knows that because of our sinfulness we need to have boundaries and limits placed upon our hearts if we are to be freed to achieve the purpose for which we were created! It is a lie of the enemy that we know ourselves better than God knows us. The truth is that God knows us and knows what we really need. Therefore, we are commanded to praise God. In fact, there is no command listed more frequently in the Scriptures than the command to "Praise the Lord!" And that's not even counting the enormous number of occurrences of the words "hallelujah" and "alleluia," which both mean "praise the Lord!"

God's requirement that we praise Him is intended to set our hearts free. Apart from God, we are not truly free. My will and heart are in bondage until I am set free by surrendering to God. Jesus said to the Jews who had believed Him, "If you hold to my teaching, you are really my disciples. Then you will know the truth, and the truth will set you free" (John 8:31,32). When some argued that they were Abraham's descendants and had never been slaves of anyone, Jesus replied, "I tell you the truth, everyone who sins is a slave to sin. Now a slave has no permanent place in the family, but a son belongs to it forever. So if the Son sets you free, you will be free indeed" (John 8:34-36). Jesus was revealing the truth that we are a slave to that which we obey. If we are obedient to sin, then we are slaves to sin. If we are obedient to God, then we are slaves to God. If we are obedient to righteousness, then we are slaves to righteousness (Romans 6:16-23). As fallen creatures, we are slaves to sin. Jesus has come to set us free from our slavery to sin that we might be free to delight in the true and living God!

Coming to Jesus, and placing faith and trust in Him, sets our hearts free. My heart continues to be set free as I come to worship and praise my Creator. God has created me for a purpose: that I might have a relationship with Him, reflect His glory, explore the marvels of His creation, and care for that creation. I am most complete as a human being when I am praising and worshiping my God, because then I am focused on the things that matter most. When I lift my heart in praise, I am following Jesus' instructions to seek first the kingdom of God (Matthew 6:33). It is only then that I have a proper perspective on life.

I have often been in situations where I was frustrated, scared, angry, apathetic, disappointed, or disillusioned, only to have things put in proper perspective when I began to praise and worship God. Although it might seem strange from our human perspective to praise God at these difficult times, these are just the times we most need the perspective that praise can give us. When I praise Him I become lost in His glory and majesty and remember that He is on His throne and in control. He is not anxious about the outcome of anything. He reigns and rules, and nothing will defeat Him. Nothing is beyond His reach. Thus praising God stills my anxieties and fears and I can see my life in the proper perspective.

When I go to the Lord, I must admit that it is too often with the purpose of gaining something from Him. Instead of giving me what I want, He gives me what I need most, which is Himself! This is the greatest gift He can give me. I come to Him like a child asking his dad for a glass of milk, and He gives me a milk truck! When we get to the end of history, when the new heavens and the new earth are revealed, we will fully realize the depth of God's graciousness. He will give Himself to us and we will be with Him. He will call us His people and He will be our God (Revelation 21:3).

In the paradox of praise and worship, I am reoriented to this reality. I am confronted with the living God, fall down before Him, and submit to His sovereignty. God is worthy of all our praise and adoration. He deserves praise from all of His creatures. And when we find Him, we truly find ourselves. Hallelujah! Praise the Lord!

Praise: The Framework for Our Lives

Psalm 147:1

REV. C. MICHAEL (MIKE) SMITH

y wife has recently taken up painting with water colors. Because she inherited an artistic gift from her mother, her work is very impressive. Her paintings give evidence of great attention to detail and careful selection of colors. One of her paintings hangs in my office, a wintry scene with a cabin and a broken-down fence, its posts still standing. The way the tall grass pushes up through the snow reminds me of scenes from my childhood in central Kentucky. The tree she added to the painting looks like it could have been in my backyard as a boy. I will sometimes sit and marvel at that tree with great delight.

When my wife finishes a painting, she signs her name to it, an indication that she considers the painting completed. Then it is ready for framing. The process of framing is very interesting to watch. She goes to a frame shop, where she is surrounded by countless options for matting and frame selection. To me, the possible combinations seem endless. Yet somehow she always seems to get it just right. First, she carefully selects a mat of just the right color to highlight the picture. With the right color mat, she says, the paintings would look better even if they didn't have a frame! Next, a frame of the right color and texture is selected. I have come to appreciate how patient she is about this process. It is critical to pick just the right frame. I have noticed that certain frames highlight the painting, while others create a less favorable effect. It can enhance the painting, overpower it, or detract from it. The frame that is chosen influences the overall effect of the whole painting.

stay close TO THE Lord

Praise is that way. It can frame your whole day. You can begin your day with praise to the Lord, continue to praise Him throughout the day, and conclude the day in praise and thanksgiving. This should be the pattern for every day! Each new day can be an opportunity to seek the Lord and praise His name. I have a good friend and mentor who told me long ago that the Lord kept him on a short tether. His advice to me was to stay close to the Lord by beginning each new day by acknowledging it as a gift from Him. Seek to honor Him throughout the day, and at day's end reflect on how you did in your walk with

God that day. I find that my prayers at the end of the day often sound something like this: "Lord, we did fairly well today, mostly You! We also had some difficulties today, mostly me. Master, help me honor You with the new day You entrust to me."

It is hard to even speak of praise as the framework of our day without speaking of singing praise to God. I find that praise usually works its way into a song. I am thankful for all those who have written songs of praise, many modeled after the Psalms, that helps me focus on praising the Lord. Throughout the book of Psalms, praise and song are often connected:

> Sing joyfully to the LORD, you righteous; it is fitting for the upright to praise him (Psalm 33:1).

> For God is the King of all the earth; sing to him a psalm of praise (Psalm 47:7).

> O my Strength, I sing praise to you; you, O God, are my fortress, my loving God (Psalm 59:17).

> Sing to the LORD, praise his name; proclaim his salvation day after day (Psalm 96:2).

> I will sing to the LORD all my life; I will sing praise to my God as long as I live (Psalm 104:33).

Of course, the Psalms themselves are actually songs. In song we are instructed to sing praise to the Lord! As I said, I am deeply appreciative of the many song writers and musicians who have written songs that help me frame my day in praise to God. I cannot play a musical instrument. In fact, the only thing I can play is the radio! But, I do enjoy singing. Songs of praise are the white lines that keep me moving straight ahead on the highway of my day. They help me stay out of life's ditches because they keep my focus on my Creator God.

I find it helpful to have a daily routine of Bible reading and prayer. I need three things for this to take place: a specific time, a specific place, and a definite agenda. If I am lacking any one of those three things, I run into problems. A place and agenda without a specific time leads me to believe I can do it "anytime," which means it often gets squeezed out by other less important things. A time and place without an agenda leads me to squander the time. An agenda and time without a place to get away and be quiet makes the time less focused. All three are important. I have found a hymnal or song sheet to be helpful to keep my mind and heart focused on "things above" (Colossians 3:1-4). It is important to find a time each day, a place to steal away to, and to know what you are going to do once you get there. And singing praise is certainly an important part of this time alone with God.

Let me encourage you to frame your day in songs of praise and adoration to God. It will be like a cup of fresh water on a dry and hot afternoon. It will be like a fresh breath of air from the Spirit of God to revive your heart and help you focus the things that really matter. Praising God will be our joy throughout all eternity. Let it be the framework for your day now, as long as the Lord gives you life and breath. So sing your praise to the Lord!

I OFFER MYSELF TO YOU

Words by Steve Green
Music by Phil Naish

I offer myself to You
Presenting every part
Pure and holy, set apart
I offer myself to You

I offer my hands to You
May labors great or small
Be done in answer to Your call
I offer my hands to You

To be holy, holy
Holy like You
To be holy, holy
Holy like You

I offer my words to You
May everything that I say
Be pleasing in Your sight, I pray
I offer my words to You

To be holy, holy
Holy like You
To be holy, holy
Holy like You

I offer my life, my praise
To You, O Lord, for endless days

To be holy, holy
Holy like You
To be holy, holy
Holy like You

To be holy, holy
Holy like You
To be holy, holy
Holy like You

The pastor of West Harpeth Primitive Baptist Church, Hewitt is a graduate of Tennessee State University and American Baptist College. A former government employee who worked with housing loans, he has lost none of his passion for community service since becoming a full-time minister. His devotions reflect his practical way of looking at how we can grow in the Christian life.

Living Sacrifices

Romans 12:1

HEWITT SAWYERS

When I think about what God desires of us, I am reminded of the old song which contains the line, "ninety-nine and a half just won't do." This is a song that suggests that we need to throw everything we are into our walk with God. Romans 12:1 exhorts us to present our bodies as "living sacrifices." This is a rather demanding call. It allows for no partial measures. It is all or nothing. *All life or no life at all.* Therefore, to present our bodies as living sacrifices means that we present our bodies *fully and completely*, or we are not presenting our bodies at all. In other words, ninety-nine and a half just won't do. Is your sacrifice living or dead? In 1 Kings 18:21, Elijah asks a question that we should ponder today:

"How long will you waiver between two opinions? If the Lord is God, follow him, but if Baal is God, follow him."

To sacrifice is to offer something that is precious to you for something you feel has a greater value. In order to have the right relationship with God, you must determine that to live your life according to your own desires is far less valuable than the reward you receive by living according to God's will. This means that you must present your body and soul fully and completely to God. Jesus illustrates this truth in Matthew 13 in His discussion of the value of the kingdom of heaven. He says that when the man in the parable understood the worth of heaven (a treasure hidden in a field), he was so overjoyed at his discovery that he sold everything he had to purchase the field. Although his wealth and holdings were precious to him, the treasure he had found was worth much more. Once you really understand the treasure to be found in a relationship with God, you'll find the same thing. When we present our bodies as living sacrifices to Him, we will find that the resulting relationship with Him is truly richer than everything that we previously considered so precious.

Of course, the essence of this offering is not just your physical body, but your *substance*. By substance I mean everything you are as a person: your mind, your body, and your spirit. God desires that you present all that you are as a sacrifice to Him. Otherwise, you are like a man who wants to go into business and asks his bank for a loan. The bank is pleased with the man's business plan and is willing to make the loan, but requires the pledge of his home as collateral. He refuses to do this, however, so he is denied approval for the loan. All of his dreams go up in smoke because he is unwilling to give up the house as collateral. You see, he had a sound business plan and had dreamed of this venture all his life, but he was not willing to go all the way. He was willing to invest his time, his talent, and his cash, but not his home. He held something back. Just as the bank required the man to hold nothing back in order to obtain financing for his business, so in the same manner God requires our bodies as living sacrifices to receive our reward.

Why does God want this kind of offering, this full surrender? Well, when God created mankind, He had a perfect relationship with him, but sin destroyed that relationship. Since that time, God has been yearning to reestablish the relationship. To do so, He has taken the initiative. God decided to give Himself, through His Son, Jesus Christ, to demonstrate how badly He wanted to reestablish that perfect relationship with man. He gave His all. So, it is a reasonable response for mankind to demonstrate commitment to God by offering ourselves as a living sacrifice. As a matter of fact, the matchless act of love shown by God in the death of His Son demands that we present our bodies as living sacrifices.

One might respond that it is too difficult to surrender completely to God, and it is. But God has never requested anything of anyone that He has not also provided the power for them to accomplish. It is by God's mercy and compassion that we are even able to make this offering. When I was first considering committing myself to full-time ministry, it was a struggle. I had a very good job that was hard to give up, but I had made the commitment to God that when He opened the doors for me to give up my secular job, I would do so. So when God reminded me of this promise almost three years ago, I can't describe the fear that came over me. My job provided me with security and prestige, and Satan whispered his "two cents worth" into my dilemma by saying, "What kind of man are you, pastor or not, that you would give up a good job and have to rely on your wife to support you and your family?" Then I attempted to bargain with God. "God," I said, "just let me get my three children out of college, and let me work long enough to pay off my mortgage so we won't have to move out of our home." Needless to say, God won the argument (as He always does), and I resigned from my job. Once I had made that commitment, the very next day my employer offered me an early retirement program. Then, about a month later, the church where I served offered me a regular salary. What did all this mean? It meant that God did not just want me to commit to full-time ministry, but He wanted me to offer myself as a living sacrifice to Him. Though it might not always come easy, the rewards are out of this world.

God has not only provided us the means to offer our bodies as living sacrifices, but also the instructions for maintaining sacrificial lifestyles. Paul warns us not to be conformed to this world. In other words, don't use the world's standard as your litmus test for sacrificial living. If you present your body a living sacrifice to God, you have the opportunity to be a *transformer* rather than a *conformer*. There was a young man at our church who wanted to be accepted by his peers so badly that he would do almost anything. As we talked one day, he said, "Pastor, I have been running with this group of guys that like each other sexually. The other night they talked me into doing some things with them that I know were not right." He was deeply troubled. I prayed with him and we studied Romans 12 together, specifically noting what Paul said about presenting your body fully and completely to God. He learned that you don't have to be a *conformer*, you can be a *transformer*. A few months later, he came back to see me. He said that since he had fully given his life over to God, he had found a joy and peace he never thought possible. Today, he is a transformer. He is now mentoring others who are struggling to break free from the homosexual lifestyle.

Since the ultimate reward of presenting yourself as a living sacrifice to God is more joyous than you can imagine, let me challenge you to consider making this investment in the Lord yourself. After all, ninety-nine and a half just isn't enough!

Offering God the Words I Speak

Psalm 19:14

HEWITT SAWYERS

"Let the words of my mouth and meditation of my heart be acceptable in thy sight, O LORD, my strength and my redeemer" (Psalm 19:14 KJV). This is a prayer many have spoken over the years. It makes clear reference to the importance of the words we speak. When I was a child, we always used to say, "Sticks and stones may break my bones, but words will never hurt me." As I grew older, I came to realize how wrong this slogan really is. You see, words arise from thoughts and thoughts arise from who and what you are. The reason words have so much power is that when they are spoken, they connect with the very core of a person's being. They have the ability to be powerfully good or powerfully bad. In order to know how words should be used, we should look carefully at this Scriptural prayer. It tells us that the meditation of our hearts—our thoughts—must be acceptable to God. Also, the words which come from these thoughts must be acceptable to God. In other words, we should determine before we open our mouths that what we are going to say is acceptable to God, because our words can be a blessing or a curse.

Proverbs 18:21 speaks of how powerful our words really are. "What you say can preserve life or destroy it. . ." (TEV). There are numerous references in Scripture that warn about the power of the tongue or the danger of careless words. Because God knew what words could do, He provided us with some wisdom on their use.

First, we should consider what and how we speak to those around us: our friends, family, or coworkers. What kinds of words do we offer and with what attitude are they expressed? Solomon points out that a gentle answer or word turns away wrath, but a harsh word stirs up anger (Proverbs 15:1). As one commentator on this verse asks us to consider: Have you ever tried to argue in a whisper? It is equally hard to argue with someone who insists on answering gently. On the other hand, a rising voice and harsh words almost always trigger an angry response. Turn away wrath and seek peace. Choose gentle words."

Second, we must understand that because of our fallen nature, we are prone to use words negatively. James writes that "all kinds of animals, birds, reptiles and creatures of the sea are being tamed and have been tamed by man, but no man can tame the tongue. It is a restless evil, full of deadly poison" (James 3:7,8). He also reminds us that though the tongue is a small part of the body, it is responsible for big things (James 3:5). We must learn to always keep our tongues (words) under control.

Finally, we must understand that how we speak to each other really matters to God. This is true because how we treat others shows what is really in our heart, and our words are a reflection of this. James exhorts us that "If anyone considers himself religious and yet does not keep a tight rein on his tongue, he deceives himself and his religion is worthless" (James 1:26). Don't be fooled. What you say, and how you say it, does make a difference. Therefore, make sure that the words you speak to others are acceptable to God. It makes a difference to Him.

Labors Great and Small

Revelation 22:12

HEWITT SAWYERS

It is just part of human nature for us to think of small things as being insignificant. Wisdom and time should have proven to us that this is incorrect, but we have paid little attention. Old sayings such as "Don't worry about the dollars. If you save the pennies, you will have the dollars" or "The journey to anywhere starts with the first step," point out that to be successful at the big things, you must first do the small things well.

A body builder would never start off with the heaviest weight he could lift when he begins his training. He would wait until he could successfully master the lighter weights before attempting the heavier ones. Many people who want to become rich fail because they have not learned how to handle small amounts of money before they try to handle a lot. Jesus illustrated this principle in the parable of the talents. To those who had taken something small and turned it into more, He said, "Well done good and faithful servant; you were faithful over a few things, I will make you ruler over many things" (Matthew 25:21 NKJV).

I have talked with many young people who are struggling to find jobs. They share with me all the things they would like to have. Once, when I asked a young man if he had a job, the answer was no. When I asked why, he said that he couldn't find one. This was my golden opportunity! I asked if I could give him a ride to a place where I knew they were hiring. He immediately asked me how much the employer was paying. Not knowing the exact pay scale, I estimated the beginning rate for that type of work to be in the area of $7.50/hour. The young man was bewildered and said he would never work for that kind of wage. Though he had no job and had no job experience, he was unwilling to start at the bottom of the pay scale. What a pity he could not see the value of working for a smaller amount in order to eventually move to a larger salary.

Unfortunately, this same attitude is alive and well both in the church and in our relationship with God. Some people will not sing in the choir unless they can be a lead vocalist. Others will not be ushers unless they can be the head usher. If we take this attitude, we will usually miss an opportunity to be a participant in building God's kingdom. We need to learn that whatever we do for the Lord, regardless of whether it is large or small, is important and necessary. What a shame if we fail to get involved just because there is not enough glory associated with the job. Jesus said that we are to work while it is day, because when night comes no one can work. Sometimes I think that God's attitude is this: If you love Me enough to do the small things well, I know I can trust you with the larger ones.

We all need to examine our hearts on this issue. We must realize that if our labor (work) is done for show, we already have our reward. Wouldn't it be better to obtain the full reward the Lord has in mind for us? In Revelation 22:12, Jesus says, "My reward is with me, and I give to everyone according to what he has done." Consider then, are you willing to do a job at home, at school, at your place of employment, or at church without worrying about who gets the credit? I truly believe that if we can do this, our labor, great or small, will be pleasing to the Lord and we will obtain the only reward that really matters.

Holiness

1 Peter 1:16

HEWITT SAWYERS

"Be holy; for I am holy." This certainly has to be one of the most challenging demands in all of the Scriptures. How can we even begin to model the holiness of God, and what is holiness anyway? Holiness, by definition, means "set apart for sacred purposes" or "separated." Perhaps the most sacred purpose for any of us is to seek God's will. If we truly follow His will for our lives, we will exhibit the kind of holiness that comes from being separated for God's use. Of course, this message is very different from the teachings of our modern culture. We are told that if it feels good, it's okay. This kind of thinking, however, causes us to conform to the world's standards rather than God's.

Unlike some other spiritual experiences, holiness is not a once and for all matter. It is a process. As Peter exhorts in 1 Peter 2:2, we must grow in grace as we feed on the milk of the Word. Holiness is a growth process. When we are saved and know we're saved, a desire should arise within us to become more like the one who gave us salvation. This is a natural spiritual movement. It might not hit us like a ton of bricks. In other words, it is unlikely that we will wake up one morning, look in the mirror, and see a holy person staring back at us. It takes time. It takes commitment.

Becoming holy starts with a deliberate and intentional choice. I recall when I was first saved, I felt there could be nothing else to it because it felt so wonderful. As the years passed, however, it startled me to find that my wants, needs, and actions were much different from what they used to be. I was changing! My focus shifted from what pleased me to what I knew pleased God. This is the sign that one is making steps toward holiness.

Holiness **IS A GROWTH** *process*

As we grow in the process of holiness, it is very helpful to find a person whom we can emulate. Of course, Jesus is the only perfect model, but there are some people who are further along in the journey than others and can be of great help to us. For me, my former pastor is a man who has helped me immensely on the road to holiness. He was helpful to me because his character demonstrated he was a man committed to the supremacy of God and the Lord, Jesus Christ. Also, he is committed to the scriptural principle of loving your neighbor as yourself. But he does not stop there, for he is always striving to demonstrate the heart of God in everything he does. So, in your quest for holiness, find such a person in your life and learn from their example.

Never allow your faults to become stumbling blocks to your efforts. God knows our imperfections. However, even with this knowledge, He still asks us to be holy as He is holy. God can take a person that, by our standards would be rejected, and make him or her shine like a freshly minted silver dollar. We all have sinned and come short of the glory of God. But since God is working with me, moving me toward holiness, it is clear that He gets joy out of dealing with persons that are less than perfect.

You have probably heard it said that holiness is next to godliness, but I say that holiness *is* godliness. The question we must ask ourselves is this: Are we willing to make a deliberate and intentional decision to be holy, and are we willing to begin the process? If so, there is no better time to start than right now. I suggest you start with prayer. Tell God you know He loves you, and express your desire to become more like Him. Then, get ready, for your change will have already begun.

SELAH

Music by Phil Naish
Instrumental

Bob Smith is a retired pastor who has had his own radio program called "Ministries for Jesus Christ" for the last ten years. He is very involved in prison ministry and serving residents in nursing homes. Bob is known to his friends as a man who is serious about prayer, a man whose prayers are obviously birthed in a deep intimacy with God. His intimate relationship with Christ shines forth in the devotions he shares in this book.

Pausing to Reflect

Psalm 42:1, 2

BOB J. SMITH

We live in a very busy and hurried world. It is easy to forget to take the time to pause and reflect on our lives.

Now that I'm retired, it is a little easier for me to find the time for pausing and reflecting. I used to be kind of a workaholic. I actually hated the thought of retiring. What would I do with all the time? Well, now that I've settled into it, it is a blessing. I've learned to sense God's presence wherever I am. When I'm out in the garden, He comes to talk with me. When I sit out on the porch, I find happiness and contentment knowing that He is with me.

In the book of Psalms, there is a word that you'll see used time and again: "selah." According to Bible scholars, this word is a musical notation that indicates an extended pause.

Since the Psalms are actually songs, the word "selah" tells us that we should pause for a moment to think about what the psalmist had written, to reflect on its meaning.

I guess when it comes to the things of God, I'm like an old cow who finishes grazing and then lies down in the pasture to chew on the food he has eaten. That's what it does for you when you take the time to pause. You can "chew on" all the events of your day and listen to what God is saying to you in your life. And you don't have to wait for retirement to do this!

I like to get up early in the morning and spend time with God. This is the best time for me to think clearly and to pray. Or sometimes in the evening I'll go stand outside and watch the sun going down. In times like these I think about my life. I remember all the big goals that I had when I got out of high school and what I planned to accomplish with my life. Well, it would be easy to let this make me feel disappointed because I'm just like everyone else: My life hasn't gone exactly according to my plan.

But what I realize when I pause to reflect is that God has had a plan for me all along. Whenever I was worried that I had missed the mark or was on the wrong trail, God was there with me. And God continues to help me. He sets things right.

But sometimes in the midst of all the demands of life it is easy for us to lose sight of His love and care for us. That is why it is always important for us to set aside some time to spend with the Lord. We can't just wait for a few spare moments to pause and reflect. We must put it in our schedule, make it part of our day. We must find time because we need God to be first in our life. Otherwise, we can sometimes travel a good long distance before we discover we are on the wrong road!

Come with me to the forty-second Psalm, and look at the first two verses:

> As the deer pants for streams of water,
> so my soul pants for you, O God.
> My soul thirsts for God, for the living God.
> When can I go and meet with God?

Picture with me, if you please, a deer being chased and running the distance of several miles. He is exhausted. He is in need of water. He cannot afford to stop because his enemy pursues him. His concern is for his very survival. And what does he need? What is it that he "pants after"? Water. He longs for it, yearns for it, desires it above all else. Without this essential element, he cannot go on.

I can certainly relate to this psalm and its message. Just like the deer I know what I must have to go on. I must have God. When I find myself in difficulties and circumstances beyond my control, I know that I must pause and drink from the inexhaustible source of spiritual power. Communion with God is essential to me.

None of us can live in our own strength. I think of the story of the woman of Samaria in John's Gospel. She came to Jacob's well at Sychar to draw water. There she met Jesus, sitting at the well. Despite all the cultural differences between them, Jesus asked her for a drink. Then He made this promise: "If you knew the gift of God and who it is that asks you for a drink, you would have asked him and He would have given you living water" (John 4:10). Jesus goes on to distinguish between the water in the well and the living water that only He could give:

> Everyone who drinks this water will be thirsty again, but whoever drinks the water I give him will never thirst. Indeed, the water I give him will become in him a spring of water welling up to eternal life (John 4:13,14).

There was an emptiness in this woman that she had never been able to satisfy. In Jesus she discovered the only thing which could quench this spiritual thirst.

If we are to find spiritual fulfillment in our lives, we must pause to drink of this same living water and take the time to reflect on the abundant life that God the Father gives us through our faith in the Lord Jesus Christ. Are you making time for "selah" in your life?

Pausing to Remember

Isaiah 43:25

BOB J. SMITH

In the previous devotion we talked about the importance of pausing to reflect upon our lives. If we let our lives rush by without giving a thought to where we are headed, we will most likely fail to find all that God has for us. One of the critical things that happens when we pause to reflect is that we remember the various ways that God has worked in our lives in the past. We remember our past sins and how God has forgiven them. We remember the tender mercies He has shown to us. We remember the promises He has written on our hearts.

Whenever I think about my past sins, I cannot do so without thinking about Jesus. About Bethlehem and His birth, His earthly ministry, the cross on the hill, His death, burial, and resurrection. What my Lord and Savior did for me makes all the difference. He has freed me from the wages of my sin.

God says: "I, even I, am he who blots out your transgressions, for my sake, and remembers your sins no more" (Isaiah 43:25). The apostle John writes of God's wonderful promise of forgiveness: "If we confess our sins, he is faithful and just and will forgive us our sins, and purify us from all unrighteousness" (1 John 1:9).

When I consider my sins, knowing that I have confessed and repented of them, I rejoice in the blessed assurance that I have been forgiven and that God remembers them no more.

Isn't that a wonderful thought? Though I can still recall my past mistakes and sins, God says that He has forgotten them! There is a purpose in my remembering them, for it helps me be on guard that I not repeat the same transgressions again. We must be realistic about our own failings! At the same time, we must not dwell upon them. Instead, let us forget those things that are behind us and reach forth for those things that are before us. We can press toward the mark for the prize of the high calling of God in Jesus Christ, always keeping in mind the grace of God.

He has FREED ME FROM THE wages of sin

Pause to remember: Consider your past sins. But time is too precious to spend more than a few moments on them.

Don't dwell upon them. They are forgiven!

When I think about the past mercies of God, I am grateful that I am still alive and still a recipient of His grace. The mercy of God comes from His grace toward us. It is one of the ways He shows us His love.

Looking back over my life, I am reminded that we are all under the blanket of God's mercies. I concur with the words of the psalmist:

> I will sing of the mercies of the Lord forever;
> with my mouth will I make known Thy faithfulness
> to all generations. For I have said, mercy shall be
> built up forever; Thy faithfulness shalt Thou estab-
> lish in the very heavens (Psalm 89:1,2 KJV).

When all else around us seems to be falling apart, we can trust in the mercy of God. David found this to be true in his life. He knew that God was the only one dependable because He was the only one truly merciful. In 2 Samuel 24:14 we find these words of David: "I am in deep distress. Let us fall into the hands of the Lord, for his mercy is great; but do not let me not fall into the hands of men." David understood that only the hands of God were truly merciful.

Pause to remember: The mercies of God are extended to every generation. That includes you and me!

When I think about God's past promises, I am grateful to be included in them. God spoke to Abraham and said,

> I will make you into a great nation
> and I will bless you.
> I will make your name great,

> and you will be a blessing.
> I will bless those who bless you,
>   and whoever curses you I will curse;
> and all peoples on earth
>   will be blessed through you (Genesis 12:2,3).

God has included you and me in these promises He made to Abraham. They were confirmed in Christ. "For no matter how many promises God has made, they are "Yes" in Christ" (2 Corinthians 1:20). When we accept Christ and His sacrificial death on behalf of lost sinners, we are placed in the body of Christ by the work of the Holy Spirit. We become part of that great nation of God's children, the universal church! That is certainly the greatest promise of all.

But our blessings don't stop there. The words of the apostle Paul catch my attention: "Praise be to the God and Father of our Lord Jesus Christ, who has blessed us in heavenly realms with every spiritual blessing in Christ" (Ephesians 1:3).

Pause to remember: God has made a place for us in His family. He is fulfilling all the promises He has given to His people. His Spirit is empowering us to be what God has called us to be. As the well-known children's song puts it, "I am a promise!"

Pause to remember.

Pause to give thanks.

Fruit Inspection

Galatians 5:22,23

BOB J. SMITH

efore a grocer puts fruit up for sale, he checks it over carefully to make sure it is good to eat. He looks over his stock and picks out the best fruit to take to market. He wants to be aware of the quality of his stock. Do you and I take the same kind of care with our spiritual lives?

We have already discussed the importance of pausing to reflect. One of the things we should do when we pause for a moment of reflection is to take an inventory of our spiritual lives. We should look closely at what our lives really look like and then compare that with what God wants our lives to look like. Of course, the purpose in this is not to make ourselves feel badly about our spiritual state, but to remember God's grace and mercy, to challenge us to keep growing in Christ.

Genesis 1:26 tells us that we were created in the image and likeness of God. But in the Garden of Eden, Adam's sin caused him to lose his likeness to the Creator. He became a creature who had the image of God, but had lost the likeness. That is the situation we all find ourselves in. We are born possessing a fallen nature, having the image of the Creator, but not His likeness.

It is only when we are clothed in the righteousness of Christ that we can regain that likeness to our Creator. His sacrifice reconnects us with God and His righteousness makes us clean. When I evaluate my spiritual life I must always remember that it is in Him that I live and move and have my being. If my spirit is cut off from God then I will only experience wretchedness. I may wander to the outermost limits of space in quest of something to satisfy my spiritual longings, but that something cannot be found except in Christ. As J. M. Pendleton writes: "The life of the soul is in its union with the blessed God." But what are the outward signs that we are being changed and that we are being transformed into the likeness of God?

We cannot rely on our personal feelings or on the evaluation of those around us. If we want an accurate assessment of where we are spiritually, we must find it in the Word of God. The Scriptures are a mirror in which we can see ourselves as we really are. When we spend time in the Word, it not only gives us clear insight but it is also used by the Holy Spirit to inspire us to strive harder to walk more closely with God.

When we pause to reflect upon our spiritual condition, it is a time both to praise God for His majesty and to judge the fruit of our lives. The Scriptures provide a helpful guide for evaluating whether we are truly living our lives in the Spirit. Galatians 5:22,23 lists the fruit of the Spirit, those qualities that should be manifest in our lives if we are truly living in the power of God. All these virtues should be manifested in our daily deportment.

Come along with me. It's fruit-checking time! Let us contemplate the fruit of the Spirit in our own lives. Could people use these words to describe you? Or are there areas where you still need to experience more of God's life being lived out in you?

Love: the greatest gift God has given us, for God is love. In it all human duty is summed up (Matthew 22:37-40).

Joy: a delight that arises within us from the consideration of a present or assured possession of a future good. It comes from believing in God's promises.

Peace: a harmonious reconciliation with God the Father through faith in Jesus Christ. This harmony should overflow into all our lives and relationships.

Longsuffering: a calm and unruffled temper, paralleling the patience God shows to each of us.

Gentleness: a God-like refusal to exact extreme penalties. We should be as gentle to others as Christ has been to us.

Goodness: the quality of character that makes its possessor lovable. It is rooted in the goodness of God.

Faith: absolute belief and trust in God. He is the only one who is fully trustworthy.

Meekness: the grace which allows us to think of ourselves no more highly than we ought to (Ephesians 4:1,2).

Self-control: the virtue of one who masters his desires and passions, especially the sensual appetites.

We can use these fruits of the Spirit as a sort of checklist to see what areas of our lives still need attention. We do this not to make ourselves feel guilty and unworthy, but to remind ourselves that God has given us a high calling *and* the power through His Spirit to live it out.

Resting and Resisting

Matthew 4:1-4

BOB J. SMITH

ometimes we can feel like our life is out of our control. Sometimes our problems control us instead of us controlling them. We have desires and appetites which seem to cry out for our attention—some of which are valid, and others which would be harmful to our spiritual life if they were fulfilled. What our flesh wants is often quite different from what our spirit knows is best for us. But whenever these appetites raise their voices, it is hard for us to ignore them.

We are not alone in the experience of being tempted by sin. Even Jesus was tempted to fulfill His fleshly desires rather than follow the path of the Spirit:

> Then Jesus was led up by the Spirit into the
> desert to be tempted by the devil. After fasting

forty days and nights, he was hungry. The tempter came to him and said, "If you are the Son of God, tell these stones to become bread." Jesus answered, "It is written: 'Man does not live on bread alone, but on every word that comes from the mouth of God'" (Matthew 4:1-4).

When Jesus was tempted He was victorious over the temptation. He knew that the best way to resist temptation was by leaning upon the power of God's Word. When the devil tempted Him to follow His appetites rather than God's path, Jesus quoted a passage of Scripture. This is a powerful tool for anyone who wants to overcome the devil's temptations.

we must KNOW THE *Word*

If we are to make use of this same tool that Jesus used against Satan, we must know the Word, believe the Word, and speak the Word. James writes, "Submit yourselves, then, to God. Resist the devil, and he will flee from you" (James 4:7). The best way of resisting the devil's lies is by pointing to truth that is contained in the Scriptures.

When we spend time in the Word we learn to think the thoughts of God. He helps us see our lives in a new way. His way is not the same as our way. That is why we need to bathe our minds in the light of the Word of God.

> For my thoughts are not your thoughts, neither are your ways my ways," declares the Lord. "As the heavens are higher than the earth, so are my ways

higher than your ways, and my thoughts than your thoughts (Isaiah 55:8,9).

The mistake that Eve made in the garden was to listen to the tempter and believe his lies instead of what God had said. She made her choice based upon the words of the tempter. She saw the fruit of the tree was good for food and she yielded to her appetite and her desire rather than obeying God's command. She listened to the wrong voice. Not only did she give in to the temptation, but she also gave the fruit to her husband to eat, thus becoming a temptress herself. What a powerful influence our own sins can sometimes have on the lives of others.

We should be thankful to God that He has given us not only the truth of the Scriptures to combat the devil's lies, but also the restraining power of the Holy Spirit, who enables us to control our appetites and conform ourselves to His will. This power is sufficient to control all the desires of the flesh.

Sometimes we fall into sin because we try to live our lives at too hectic of a pace and cannot find room for spending time with God. When we are not spending time in His presence, not partaking regularly of the Word of God, we are much more susceptible to the lure of our sinful nature.

God set a pattern for us by commanding Israel to observe the Sabbath as a day of rest. It was a God-ordained call to slowing our pace, to setting some time aside for what is really most important in our lives. Jesus Himself knew the importance of rest. In Mark 6:31 we hear Jesus say this to His disciples: "Come with me by yourselves to a quiet place and get some rest." Jesus knew the importance of rest. When our bodies are tired out we lack the resources we need to fight off temptation.

Woe unto us if we become too busy to give our bodies the proper amount of rest. No matter how sincere we are, no matter how noble the goal, we cannot neglect to find time to rest. God wants us to take care of the earthly house He has given us. This is the problem with becoming a workaholic. Jesus often withdrew into the wilderness to pray (Luke 5:16). Since even Jesus found it necessary to spend time alone in prayer, how much more necessary is it for us to slow down our pace and find time to pray?

Oh, that we would store up the Word of God in our minds and apply it daily to our lives. Oh, that we would slow down our hectic pace and find the time to pray and enjoy fellowship with our blessed Savior. If we do these things, we will find victory over sin and be able to control our passions rather than letting them control us.

LISTEN

*Words and Music
by Rob Mathes*

I can read Your Word
But I may not know Your mind
I can think I hear Your voice
But I might be running blind
And I need You
In this particular situation
Yes, I need You
Like I always do
So I will wait in quiet, earnest anticipation
I will listen to You

Listen close
Listen deep
Way beyond the silence
Trembling at what You speak
I will pray Thy Kingdom come
I will pray Thy will be done
And I will listen

I can talk all night
To the ones who say they know
I can take their advice
And where they point, I can go
But I need You to give my heart direction
Yes, I need You
Like I always do
So I will wait in quiet, earnest anticipation
I will listen to You

Yes, I need You
To give my heart direction
And I know that You will see me through
So I will wait in quiet, earnest anticipation
I will listen to You

Until his recent death, Bill Lane was considered one of the foremost living New Testament scholars. Although this Harvard Ph.D. spoke 16 languages and wrote a number of highly esteemed Bible commentaries, he was best known for his unaffected humility and his profound insights into Scripture. The other members of Empty Hands unanimously attest to the powerful impact he had on their lives through his words and through the testimony of his character. These devotions are the last writing he produced, just days before his death. They are evidence of a profound mind fueled by a simple faith in the love of God.

Living in the Eye of the Hurricane

Psalm 46

WILLIAM LANE

*O*ur world is a very noisy place. We are surrounded by the incessant clatter of machines, the wailing of fire trucks and police cars, the constant buzz of radios and televisions, and the excited screams of children on playgrounds. No matter where we go, we are surrounded by constant clamor. As we see in Psalm 46, even creation itself joins in the noisy chorus: "the earth give[s] way and the mountains fall into the heart of the sea…its waters roar and foam and the mountains quake with their surging" (Psalm 46:2,3). These words convey to us an impression of an expanding, exploding chaos. Don't our lives sometimes feel that way, too? In the midst of all this tumult, where do we find shelter from the storm? How do we live in the eye of the hurricane?

Psalm 46 holds the answer we need for dealing with the hurricanes in our personal lives. It reminds us that only in God's power can we find our security. When it was first written, this psalm was used as a confessional hymn, a reminder to God's people of where their confidence and security could truly be found. They would recite it aloud in unison, a hymn of praise giving thanks for God's faithfulness. Since God Himself is our protection, the psalm reminds us, "we will not fear" (Psalm 46:2). He will protect us from all that comes against us, whether it be natural disasters, enemies who rise to attack us, the collapse of nations, or just the collapse of our own personal world. As the psalmist notes the crises of life, he is buoyed by a constant refrain: "God is our refuge and strength, a very present help in trouble" (Psalm 46:1 NASB). Those who listen for the voice of God above the noise of the world can be confident that He extends His care and protection toward them.

in God's **POWER CAN WE FIND** *our security*

In powerful imagery, the psalmist points to the instability and insecurity of life in this world if we are left to our own resources. He calls to mind volatile events in nature such as earthquakes, tidal waves, avalanches, or the eruption of volcanoes. These serve to remind us of how helpless we really are in the face of such natural catastrophes. They show us that we are ultimately helpless. That we are ultimately weak. Yet, despite our human powerlessness, the psalmist is confident. "We will not fear," he writes, "though the earth give way" (verse 2). Though we have no control over the forces of nature, God does!

Similarly, the fractured record of human history shows us that we cannot place our confidence in even the best laid plans of human ingenuity. We see the ambitions of scheming human leaders, eager to write their signature in the dust of human history. We see nations rise and fall, kingdoms come and go. But behind all the maneuvering of nations and leaders is the action of God on behalf of His people. He will execute judgment and bring peace. We are invited to "Come and see the works of the LORD, the desolations he has brought on the earth. He makes wars cease to the ends of the earth; he breaks the bow and shatters the spear, and burns the shields with fire" (verses 8,9). Our God is the God who acts, and His voice, heard above the din of battle, interprets His mighty acts for any who will listen. Only in His presence can security be found in this insecure and noisy world. He is "our refuge and strength, an ever-present help in trouble" (verse 1).

This psalm encourages us to remember that God is our protector in the storms of life. When the psalmist breaks into song, he sings, "God is our refuge" (verse 1) and "the God of Jacob is our stronghold" (verses 7,11 NASB). While excavating in the Holy Land, archaeologists discovered that one of the most common and most important structures of any city or town was a sturdy stone tower. This tower was built so that citizens could flee there for refuge whenever the walls of the settlement began to be penetrated and when the enemy was poised to pour in through the breech. That is the vivid image behind the psalmist's confession that "God is our refuge and strength, our stronghold." It is the same image that inspired Martin Luther to pen his great hymn, "A Mighty Fortress is Our God!" It reminds us that God is there to protect and shelter us whenever the world begins to close in upon us.

Certainly we live with chaos pressing upon us at all times. But the psalmist reminds us that God is the creator, the One who fashioned order out of the primeval chaos. When He created the world, God only needed to utter a command and chaos was replaced by order. So, when the earth shakes beneath our feet there is no reason to be afraid. God has already conquered the chaos! Because He controls both nature and history, the threat of chaos may be faced without fear. When everything seems to be coming apart in our lives, we can know that our stronghold remains firm. The very worst experiences of chaos in our lives—living in the very midst of the hurricane—can be overcome by the One who subdues chaos. His protecting hand will keep us safe, helping us find that still point of peace in the eye of the hurricane.

But it is only the person who hearkens to the voice of God above the noise of the world who will perceive the hand and presence of God in the midst of the chaos of life. We have a prophetic word of promise that is the source of our hope: "Be still, and know that I am God; I will be exalted among the nations, I will be exalted in the earth!" (verse 10 NKJV).

We need to cultivate within our hearts the silence that allows us to listen to the voice of God, rather than the noise of the world. In the silence of prayer God speaks to us, even as we speak to Him. Then we will *know* that God is God. It is in the quietness of our hearts that we experience His presence and power. We might paraphrase this verse as follows: "Relax in the certainty that I am God, and that I will be exalted among the nations. As I bring peace on the earth, so I bring peace to the human heart. Relaxing in the conviction that I am God will enable you to listen to My voice rather than to the voice of your fears."

To know God in this way is to know Him experientially. He is not a theological abstraction, but One with whom we may enter into relationship. To know Him in this way is to allow His peace to settle down upon us and quiet our pounding hearts. It is to experience God as our security and stability when we are living in the midst of the hurricane.

As the song "Listen" suggests, God becomes very real to us when we bend our ear toward Him.

> Listen close.
> Listen deep.
> Way beyond the silence,
> Trembling at what You speak.

This kind of listening gives us the confidence to state boldly: "I will pray Thy kingdom come, I will pray Thy will be done, and I will listen." For it is in the act of listening that we hear the reassurance that the One who is our stronghold cares deeply about every struggle of our noisy and chaotic lives. Truly, "the LORD of hosts is with us; the God of Jacob is our stronghold" (verses 7,11 NASB).

The Urgency of Listening

Hebrews 3:7-11

WILLIAM LANE

The book of Hebrews is one of my favorite books in the whole of Scripture. I often think of it as a sermon rooted in real life. It addresses men and women who are just like ourselves, people who discover that they can be very easily thrown off course by circumstances over which they have no control. We are all emotionally fragile and easily undone by the pain and confusion that so often are a part of our lives. Life is not always easy, even when we are walking in close fellowship with God. The song "Listen" reflects the feeling of being confused and uncertain in the face of all our struggles:

> I can read Your Word
> But I may not know Your mind

> I can think I hear Your voice
> But I might be running blind
> And I need You
> In this particular situation

If you have ever felt yourself overwhelmed by the harsh realities of life, then the book of Hebrews contains a sermon you need to hear.

The insistent question of the writer of Hebrews is this: *Will you be faithful?* Jesus is our example of One who was faithful to God in all He was sent to do (Hebrews 2:17–3:6). That is a difficult example to try to follow, but we are reminded that we show ourselves to be a member of God's household if we also prove to be faithful (Hebrews 3:6). The question is addressed anew to us today: Will you be faithful?

In exhorting us to faithfulness, the writer of Hebrews cites Psalm 95:7-11 and connects that Scripture with the present experience of his friends in the family of God. There are at least four reasons why he chooses this particular passage, a passage which is probably unfamiliar to us.

First, the passage would have been well-known to his friends. In the first century, it served as the call to worship every Sabbath evening when the synagogue community gathered together: "Today, if you hear his voice, do not harden your hearts" (Psalm 95:7,8). Week after week, these urgent words were used to call those who attended the synagogue to listen intently to the voice of God in Scripture.

Second, this passage was a sober reminder of the past unfaithfulness of the people of God. The Israelites had experienced God's faithfulness in the exodus and His provision in the wilderness, but at critical moments in their history, they refused to believe God's word of promise. Yet, despite their lack of faith, God had always proven Himself faithful. This is the reminder we need when our faithfulness wavers. We could easily summarize Psalm 95:7-11 in this way: "Let us remember the faithfulness of God, and be faithful and attentive when He speaks."

Third, this passage stresses how important it is to listen attentively to the voice of God. The book of Hebrews underscores this emphasis: "We must pay the closest attention to what we have heard, so that we do not drift off course" (Hebrews 2:1). Psalm 95 brings this urgent condition before us in a powerful way.

Finally, this passage drives home the peril of unbelief and the tragic cost of faithlessness. It concludes with the sober pronouncement: "So I declared an oath in my anger, 'They shall never enter my rest'" (Psalm 95:11). The consequence of refusal to listen to God's voice was to be excluded from the promised rest He offered.

When the writer of Hebrews makes reference to Psalm 95, it is clear that he is interpreting it in relation to a defining event in the history of Israel, recorded in Numbers 13 and 14. The Israelites had traveled from Egypt to Kadesh-Barnea, a point of entrance into Canaan. Having experienced God's faithfulness in the exodus from Egypt, the crossing of the Red Sea, and the pilgrimage through the desert, there was every reason to expect God's work on their behalf to be climaxed by entrance into the Promised Land. The sense of imminent possession of the land was prompted by God's instruction to Moses: "The Lord said to Moses, 'Send some men to explore the land of Canaan, which I am giving to the Israelites'" (Numbers 13:1,2). Those who were sent into Canaan were on a spy mission to gather intelligence concerning the land and its population (Numbers 13:17-20).

After forty days, the spies returned from their mission with abundant evidence of the fruitfulness of the Promised Land. It truly did flow with milk and honey! But the spies also reported that it was a land that struck terror in their hearts. The people who lived there were firmly entrenched in impregnable cities. There were even giants in the land, and in comparison to them the Israelites "seemed like grasshoppers." Their conclusion was that "the land we explored devours those living in it" (Numbers 13:28-33).

But this majority report was challenged by Joshua and Caleb. They were convinced that the land could be conquered, and that God's presence and promise would provide the margin of victory. Nevertheless, the people were not convinced by the optimism of Joshua and Caleb, and a deep spirit of despair settled upon them. They discussed the possibility of electing new leadership and returning to Egypt, and even talked about stoning Joshua and Caleb, who had warned them not to rebel against the Lord. The people responded to the Lord with hardness of heart (Numbers 14:10).

What is "hardness of heart"? It means treating God with contempt by refusing to believe in His promises. It means choosing to listen to human voices of despair rather than listening to the voice of God. This tragic story was called to mind every time the Jewish people gathered for worship. It is the historical background to the somber warning in Hebrews 3:7,8: "Today, if you hear his voice, do not harden your hearts as you did in the rebellion, during the time of testing in the desert."

The writer of Hebrews wanted to bring this painful scene into the consciousness of his friends. He does so by casting the formula from Psalm 95 into the present tense: "So, then, *as the Holy Spirit is saying,* 'Today, if you hear his voice, do not harden your hearts'" (Hebrews 3:7,8). The stress falls on the fact that the Holy Spirit is speaking these words right now. In this striking way, the writer of Hebrews brings the tragic sequence of events at Kadesh-Barnea before his friends, who like the song writer, were "running blind."

In applying the ancient story to Christians he draws two significant conclusions: First, in the presence of Scripture, we are confronted with a fresh moment of biography for every one of us (Hebrews 3:7-9). The focus of Psalm 95 and Hebrews 3 is on the word "today"—the present moment! "Today" is a fresh moment of biography for every one of us because our response to God's voice "in this particular situation" will inevitably shape our story. God is speaking now—through the text of Scripture and the word of preaching. Are we listening?

Second, in the presence of Scripture we are confronted with the Spirit's passionate plea (Hebrews 3:7,8). The writer of Hebrews deliberately uses the present tense ("The Holy Spirit *is saying*") to bring a past word of Scripture into the present experience of the people of God. The Spirit *is* speaking, pleading passionately, right now! Therefore, in the present moment we are faced with two options: the option of the hardened heart or the option of the heart responsive to the voice of God.

Let us not make the mistake of allowing other voices—our fears, our desires, the expectations of others—to drown out the passionate call of the Spirit of God. The Spirit pleads passionately because God cares passionately for us. To whose voice are you attentive today?

An Attitude of Expectation

Mark 4:3-9

WILLIAM LANE

*O*ur children are a constant reminder of how much we want to be heard. During a recent trip to the mall I saw a very familiar sight: a young child tugging on her mother's skirt, trying desperately to get her attention. But no matter how hard she tried, she just couldn't seem to get mom to notice her and attend to her needs. It reminded me of my own sons and their importunate pleadings. I can recall what would happen every time I returned from a trip and was met by my family at the gate. We would all climb into the car, the boys taking their place in the back seat. All the way home, first one, and then the other, would pound on my shoulder with his small fists until I turned around to listen to what he had to say. Of course, just having returned from my trip, I had stories of my own and wasn't listening as closely to theirs as I should have! When I made eye contact with them and asked what they needed, the answer would often be a little smile and the phrase, "I forgot." What they really wanted more than anything else—even more than the chance to tell their story—was my undivided attention.

Our culture spends a lot of energy participating in what I sometimes refer to as "the dialogue of the deaf." Voices from every quarter clamor for our attention. But everyone is speaking and no one seems to be listening. We speak in the expectation that we will be heard, but we rarely take the time to listen even to those nearest us—their hopes, their fears, their needs, their dreams. We live in a deaf culture and have not developed the habit of really listening to others. As a consequence, we have become impoverished, shut up to the sound of our own voice and to the poverty of our own thoughts. Where is the friend who will simply listen to us, and who will respond "I *hear* you"?

"*I HEAR You*"

I smile wryly as I recall a moment from years ago when I had my nose buried in the newspaper, oblivious to the needs of my wife. She had patiently waited for me to return from my day at the office, and here I was completely ignoring her! Finally, she leapt upon my lap, tossed the newspaper aside, threw her arms around my neck, and said, "Remember me? I'm your wife!" I am embarrassed when I think of all the times that I failed to really listen to her. I deeply regret these times. It takes some of us a long time to learn that the best way you can show someone you love them is by listening to them.

Isn't it strange that, although all our human relationships continually remind us that each of us wants someone to listen to us, it never occurs to us that God is crying out to be heard in a multitude of ways. Prior to their entrance into the Promised Land, God spoke to the children of Israel, identifying Himself as the Lord. His words became the central confession of Israel, known as the *Shema* (taken from the Hebrew word which means to hear or listen): "Listen, O Israel, the Lord our God, the Lord is one" (Deuteronomy 6:4). Growth in our relationship with God begins with our determination to listen to Him.

The command to listen is sounded again and again throughout the Old Testament: "Listen to me, O Jacob, Israel, whom I have called: I am he; I am the first and I am the last... Come together, all of you and listen"(Isaiah 48:12,14). Throughout the writing of the great prophets Isaiah, Jeremiah, and Ezekiel we find the repeated formula that introduces an oracle from God: "Hear the word of the Lord!"

The same emphasis on listening is a characteristic of the ministry of Jesus. He really listened to people, attempting to connect with their deepest needs. Consider, for example, His parables. The parables were extended comparisons, making known some important aspect of truth which could be grasped more clearly by comparing it to something that was already familiar to its hearers. So, for example, Jesus speaks of planting, growth, and harvest to the Galileans, who were farmers themselves, or He speaks of the effect of putting a pinch of yeast into a bowl of bread dough to women who baked bread every day. What we see in a parable is that there is an analogy between experiences in the natural realm and redemptive truth. By contemplating the familiar in our own circumstances, we gain insight into the unfamiliar, namely, the Kingdom of God.

The parable of the sower is one of the stories which Jesus uses to help His hearers understand an important truth about the kingdom. And this parable is framed at the beginning and end with a solemn call to listen (Mark 4:3,9). With this call, Jesus invites His audience into a familiar situation and calls them to make a judgment concerning it. He also warns that there may be more to the parable than appears upon its surface. Sometimes superficial listening will cause us to miss the point!

Why did Jesus use parables to teach His disciples? Why not just give them a straightforward theology lesson? Isn't it because Jesus really wanted to get our attention and He knew that a story was the very best way to do that? The parables are riddles told to keep the people open and intrigued with the message Jesus proclaimed. They make difficult ideas more understandable. In them, God is crying out to be heard. Jesus is tugging at our pant leg, pulling at our skirt, asking us to listen. Are we prepared to really pay attention?

Let us respond as the writer of the song:

> Yes, I need You
> Like I always do
> So I will wait in quiet, earnest anticipation,
> I will listen to You

May that become the prayer of each one of us.

Listen and Obey

1 Samuel 15

WILLIAM LANE

When we think about how much God has done for us, there is something within us that causes us to want to do something for Him in return. But what can we possibly do that will please Him? What is it that will most delight His heart? What does He really want from us?

The answer is simple: obedience.

I have always thought that the story of Saul's disobedience, recorded in 1 Samuel 15, is one of the most eye-opening passages in the whole Old Testament. In recording for us the circumstances that led to God's rejection of Saul as the king of Israel, this story shows us the terrible consequences of failing to respond to God with complete obedience.

Let's face it. God exerts an absolute claim upon us. He has a right to. We belong to Him because He is not only our creator, but also our redeemer. We are not free agents who can simply do whatever we please. But our obedience is something which pleases Him.

> Does the LORD delight in burnt offerings and
>   sacrifices as much as in obeying the voice
>   of the LORD?
> To obey is better than sacrifice,
> And to listen is better than the fat of rams
> (1 Samuel 15:22).

The key to this prophetic word is the relationship between listening and obedience. The accent in the entire story, in fact, falls on listening to and obeying the voice of God. It begins with the command to listen: "Samuel said to Saul, 'I am the one the LORD sent to anoint you king over his people Israel; so listen now to the message from the LORD'" (1 Samuel 15:1). The message they received was this: God had chosen to punish the Amalekites for the way they had treated Israel. Israel was to go into battle against them and *totally destroy them*. Saul responded to this message by mustering all his armed men for battle, but his obedience was only partial. He did not completely destroy them. He spared Agag, their king "and the best of the sheep and cattle, the fat calves and lambs—everything that was good. These [Saul and the army] were unwilling to destroy completely, but everything that was despised and weak they totally destroyed" (1 Samuel 15:9). Satisfied that he had heeded God's instructions, Saul made his way to Mount Carmel, where he set up a monument in his own honor, and then led his troops, the captured king, and the herds of sheep and cattle to Gilgal, where he intended to sacrifice them to the Lord.

But God was not pleased with this act of partial obedience. Samuel received a word from the Lord that He was grieved that He had made Saul king "because he has turned away from me and has not carried out my instructions" (1 Samuel 15:11). Samuel fully understood what this meant: God had rejected Saul.

Listen **CLOSE, LISTEN** *deep*

When Samuel finally caught up with Saul at Gilgal, the king feigned ignorance of his folly. He greeted the aged prophet warmly, "The LORD bless you! I have carried out the LORD's instruction."

"What, then, is this bleating of sheep in my ears? What is this lowing of cattle that I hear?" Samuel asked.

Saul answered confidently, "The soldiers brought them from the Amalekites; they spared the best of the sheep and cattle to sacrifice to the LORD your God, but we totally destroyed the rest" (1 Samuel 15:13-15). Samuel cut off the conversation with a single word, "Stop!" In other words, don't tell me what the soldiers did. "Why did you not obey the LORD? Why did you pounce on the plunder and do evil in the eyes of the LORD?" (1 Samuel 15:19).

"But I did obey the LORD," Saul protested. "I went on the mission the LORD assigned me. I completely destroyed the

Amalekites and brought back Agag their king. The soldiers took sheep and cattle from the plunder, the best of what was devoted to God, in order to sacrifice them to the Lord your God at Gilgal" (1 Samuel 15:20,21). Resorting to rationalization and shifting the blame from himself to the soldiers, Saul sought to excuse the fact that *he* had not listened to the voice of God! The result of failing to listen to God's voice will always be disobedience.

This is the setting for those powerful words in 1 Samuel 15:22: "To obey is better than sacrifice, and to listen is better than the fat of rams."

The two statements of this prophetic couplet are parallel. The verb "to obey" is complemented by the verb "to listen," even as the term "sacrifice" is echoed in the phrase "the fat of rams." Do you see the direct correlation between hearing and obeying? This correlation would have been even clearer to Saul and Samuel than it is to us, because in the Hebrew language the verb "to obey" is an intensified form of the verb "to hear." They share a common root. Obedience, then, begins with the readiness to listen.

The repeated refrain in the song "Listen" makes this point well. To say, "I will listen to You" is to affirm "I will obey You." God is earnestly speaking into our lives. Let us respond, "I will listen to You," confident that earnest listening is the condition for the obedience which so pleases the heart of God. And if our heart's desire is to please God, we must make the obedience which grows out of listening our first priority.

MORNING HAS BROKEN

Words by Eleanor Farjeon
Traditional Tune

orning has broken, like the first morning,
Blackbird has spoken, like the first bird.
Praise for the singing! Praise for the morning!
Praise for them springing, fresh from the Word!

Sweet the rain's new fall, sunlit from heaven,
Like the first dew fall on the first grass.
Praise for the sweetness of the wet garden,
Sprung in completeness, where His feet pass.

Hallelujah, Hallelujah, Hallelujah!

Mine is the sunlight, mine is the morning.
Born of the one light Eden saw play!
Praise with elation, praise every morning,
God's recreation of the new day!
God's recreation of the new day!

Walter Amos is the pastor of Franklin Primitive Baptist Church. His mother, who faithfully prayed for him during his years of rebellion from the Lord, is now one of the members of his congregation. He is retired from a job with the federal government and served in the U.S. Army (including a stint in Korea). Since his call to the ministry, he has been a student at Franklin Bible Institute. As he shares in his devotions, Walter has learned to find the grace and faithfulness of God in the midst of life's struggles and temptations.

Prayer Changes Me

Mark 1:35

ELDER WALTER M. AMOS, JR.

When I wake up every morning, the first thing I do is to roll over out of bed and straight onto my knees. Then I begin to pray. I thank God for watching over me during the night and enabling me to open my eyes to see a new day. I've been doing this for long enough that by now it's just a natural response. It is as much a part of my morning routine as putting on my pants! Just like I wouldn't think of going out without wearing my pants, so I wouldn't want to go out into the new day without starting it with prayer.

Without prayer, sometimes my day will start to unravel. Just the other morning, I woke up very early. In fact, it was still dark out. But I was feeling pretty awake and so I sat up on my bed for a minute and then got up and went to use the bathroom. All of a sudden I was overcome by all the worries of the day to come. My day just wasn't starting right! So what did I do? I climbed right back into bed, then immediately rolled out onto my knees. I had to begin my day with prayer! I could not live without its power in my life. I am a personal witness of how it can change your life.

I didn't always know the power of prayer. During my formative years I didn't really know God. My life was centered around alcohol, women, and cars. My father was a pastor, but I worked hard to avoid God's interference in my life. But my lifestyle sent me into a downward spiral. My addictions came to have so much control over me that I wasn't really free.

That is when I discovered the help offered by Alcoholics Anonymous. AA helped prayer become more real for me. It told me I needed God and that I could reach out for His help. It directed me back to God and made Him more personal and real and available. When I needed Him most, He was there.

I am still learning a lot about prayer and the different ways we can pray.

Sometimes prayer is just being with Jesus, feeling His presence in my life, and just spending quiet time with Him. Sometimes I can just be sitting in my house and feel His presence with me. I'll be sitting here and I'll say, "Well Lord, are You going to tell me something? Are You going to say something to me?" And then I can hear Him say in response, "No, I just want to be with you. I just want you to know that I love you."

Sometimes prayer is a conversation with God, just Him and me talking about my life and His plans for me. I can be totally honest with Him, just like David was in the Psalms.

Sometimes prayer is asking God to meet my needs. I've learned that it's okay to ask. This was an important lesson. For a number of years I carried around a lot of bitterness about something that happened when I tried out for the high school football team. I was very excited about making the team, but my school had such a small budget that each team member had to buy their own shoes. I told my dad that I needed football shoes,

When I NEEDED HIM MOST, he was there

so he went out and bought me a used pair. They were serviceable, but they looked at little worse for the wear. Unfortunately, everyone else got brand new shoes from their parents, so my old shoes really stood out. I was embarrassed and bitter, and I held onto that bitterness for years. One day I decided to make amends with my father, so I said to him, "Daddy, why did you buy me those old football shoes instead of getting some new ones for me?" He got a surprised look on his face and answered, "You just said you needed football shoes. You didn't say anything about new ones!" From this incident I learned the important lesson of asking God specifically for what I need. God wants me to open up my heart to Him and let Him know what I need and desire.

193

When we pray, God answers. But sometimes God asks us to cooperate with Him to accomplish His will for our lives. When we pray, God gives us the strength and health and the days we need to do what needs to be done to get that prayer answered, because part of it may be our own responsibility.

Perhaps more than anything else, prayer helps us keep our focus on God. We're just like Peter, who, when Jesus called to him, was able to walk on water. Until, that is, Peter took his eyes off Jesus and started looking at the waves that surrounded him. Then he started to sink. Prayer helps us keep our focus where it needs to be: on the Savior. He keeps us afloat in the sea of all our problems.

It's important to remember that prayer is not just about me talking to God. It's also about me learning to listen to Him. One of the sisters at the church I pastor constantly reminds me that I need to wait on the Lord in prayer and not run off in my own direction. "Slow down," she will say, "and listen to God."

That's good advice and the best way to let prayer begin to change me.

Grateful for God's Creation

Psalm 95:1-5

ELDER WALTER M. AMOS, JR.

As a child, I can remember visiting my grandparents' farm. I always loved to visit them in the summer. I'd lived in the city all my life, so I really enjoyed going out to their place in the country. How I used to love to climb up on a grassy knoll overlooking the farm, kick off my shoes, and lie back in the sweet clover. I'd stare up into the blue sky and listen to the sound of the birds and the neighing of the horses. I always felt a strange sort of peace in those moments. And though I didn't fully understand it as a child, I think I felt something of the presence of God's love reaching out to me.

I still love the outdoors today. I like to watch the sun rising in the morning and love to stare up into the stars at night. One of my hobbies is fishing. I enjoy its challenge and its slow pace. But one of the things I most enjoy about fishing is the solitude. It makes me feel so close to God. Just out there in the boat alone with Him and with nature. I love being able to communicate with God out there in the wide open spaces. He doesn't even have to come through the roof of a building to get to me!

Ultimately, the beauty of creation points us toward the only One who is truly beautiful, our Lord Jesus Christ. All the beauty we see is His reflection.

The beauty of nature always makes me think about God and His ways. There are so many parables of God's work in our lives that can be found in nature. Here are a couple of my favorites.

It makes ME FEEL CLOSE to God

Our life is like a tree. Just as the tree is nourished by drawing water up into its roots, so the Word of God and His love provide the strength and nourishment we need to grow strong. If we are going to grow, we need God's love to flow through us. He gives us the strength we need to be the people He desires us to be. When the tree of our life bears fruit, it is the fruit of a changed heart. God works on us from the inside out. But growth is hard, and sometimes we meet difficulties along the way. Too often, when someone or something shakes the tree that is our life, we are afraid we will fall. Let's not forget that it is only in Christ that we can find a stable place to stand. Our roots must go deep into God's Word, just as the roots of a tree must go deep into the earth.

Our life is also like a stream of water. It is a stream which flows from the heart of God and brings refreshment and cleansing to our lives. And just as that stream continues to flow, so should our love flow from God into the lives of others. We can become channels of God's love and mercy.

Actually, even dirt makes me think of the spiritual life. Our sin makes us dirty inside, in need of the cleansing that only God can bring. We cannot deal with that "dirt" all by ourselves. We need His power, His grace.

We know the reality of a loving and powerful God by the signs that are all around us. He has created the mountains, He makes the trees grow, He cuts rivers out through the rocks with His hands, and He carves out the valleys. No man can do all that! The same kind of power He shows in His creation is the power He will bring into our lives. That power is shown in no more amazing way than in the fact that He forgives our sins and makes us new creations in Christ.

We think sometimes that God's creative work has stopped, but it hasn't. He is still working. As the song says, "Morning has broken, like the first morning." Day after day, He offers us His gifts.

Each New Day

Lamentations 3:22,23

ELDER WALTER M. AMOS, JR.

The song "Morning Has Broken" is a great reminder that each day is a fresh new creation from the hand of God. Each day is unlike the one before it. Each day reminds us of those first days of creation, when God brought new beauties into the world. Each day is a new opportunity to be thankful for all the wonderful gifts that God has given us.

When I first awake in the morning, I always try to remember to say, "Thank You, Jesus, for a brand new day!" God is still in the business of creating. The changes that we see in our world all happen because of God. And no day is the same as the one that came before it.

Each new day is a new beginning. One of the powerful lessons I learned from AA was to take "one day at a time."

We can't spend all our time worrying about the future. Each new day we learn more about how we should live our lives and each new day gives us new opportunities to grow in our relationship with God. God can take every negative in our life and turn it into a positive as He heals and delivers us.

Each new day should be filled with thankfulness for His grace and for His answers to our prayers.

Each new day we can remember how far we have come by the grace of God.

Each new day we need God to help us make the next step in our lives.

Being born again means we get a new start. The old person within us is dead and the new person is clean, made white as snow. On this new day we are a new creation. Sure we are going to make mistakes. But God can use us anyway. Even with the sinful things we do, He still allows us to move forward. If we stumble and fall, He picks us up and lets us start all over again.

God doesn't leave us in the dark. Each new day He shows us everything we need to know just at the time when we're ready for it. Each new day we must listen to God and be available to Him. When we fail to go forward in obedience, we miss some of the blessings He has in store for us. After all, even though we are new creatures, we still struggle with the flesh. And the flesh will always try to overcome the good that God intends for us. Satan makes everything look so good on the outside, but when we really see things as they are, we learn that we have been sold a lie. God's blessings are far superior to anything the world can offer.

After coming back to the church following a number of years of rebellion against God, I found that I was always waiting for some "bolt of lightning" to strike and show me what God had in store for my life. But it wasn't long before I learned that I didn't need any bolts of lightning. What I really needed was to simply be aware on a daily basis of what God was doing in my life. I needed to learn to look for the small ways He was blessing me and guiding me. Those small steps add together to make up the path He has for me. The steps of a good man are ordered by the Lord.

Therefore, we should embrace each new day as it comes. As I sometimes have to remind myself: Yesterday is history, tomorrow is mystery, and all we really have is today! Let us be grateful for today and for all its blessings. Everything we have really belongs to God. Each new day is a gift from His hand.

Show Me the Book

2 Timothy 3:16,17

ELDER WALTER M. AMOS, JR.

The church today is full of a lot of crazy ideas: preachers preaching all kinds of strange teachings and pews full of people with all kinds of false concepts about God. Many seem more concerned with tickling the ears of their congregation than with standing firm for God's truth. So where can we go to get the truth about God? What is really dependable in this day and age when so few things can be counted upon? There is only one answer: the Bible!

Whenever someone starts to tell me about some new idea they have about God, I just look them straight in the eye and say, "Show me the Book!" If it can't be found in the Bible, then it probably isn't worth hearing about! The kind of pride that says we can figure it all out for ourselves is the kind of pride that leads straight to hell. At its heart, the message of the Scriptures is pretty simple. Even a spiritual baby can understand the basic teaching of the gospel. All we have to do is sit down and read.

I've often heard ministers say to "try the spirit by the Spirit." But unless you try the spirit by the Word, you can fall into deception. If you can't find support for your ideas in the Scriptures, then you cannot claim to be led by God's Spirit. Satan will fool you in a heartbeat. He can even quote Scripture to you, though he always takes it out of context.

It's easy for us to get diverted from the path God has for us. We forget how slick and clever Satan is and how much he wants to distract us from God's path. We must always remember that we cannot fight Satan in our own strength. We need the Word of God to counter his lies.

As a preacher, I must always remind myself of this: Don't preach a little bit of Walter and a little bit of Jesus. The only message that will save souls and heal lives is the message of Jesus Christ. And we find that message in the Word of God.

Because the message of the Bible is so powerful, we must take it seriously and handle it with care. As 2 Timothy 3:16,17 says, "All Scripture is God-breathed and is useful for teaching, rebuking, correcting and training in righteousness, so that the man of God may be thoroughly equipped for every good work." Because of its spiritual power, we must respect the Word of God. This means that we must correctly understand the context of the passage we are studying, not just use it as a tool to get across our own ideas.

We need to take the message of the Bible seriously. If God said it, He meant it. It is our guide for life. Therefore, it is not enough just to read the Bible. We must believe it and obey it. For example, the Bible teaches us that it is important to tithe a portion of your income to God. Basically, God says, "If you give Me the first 10 percent so I can have meat in My house, I will open the windows of the storehouse for you." This was not an easy thing for me to do at first, but I knew it was what the Bible required. So I started tithing and I haven't had a broke day since! I haven't had a car note or fallen behind in my bills. I haven't missed a meal and I haven't been without clothes. I obeyed the Word of God and God blessed me.

Let's not play games with the Bible. Read it just as it is and do it just like it says.

Show me the Book!

IN THE MORNING

*Words and Music
by Steve Green*

In the morning, deep calls to deep
In the morning, You quietly speak
In the morning, You find those who seek
In the morning.

In the morning, I bring my request
In the morning, each care is confessed
In the morning, You quiet unrest
In the morning.

Hallelujah, Hallelujah, Hallelujah

In the morning, I listen and wait
In the morning, faith anticipates
In the morning, You make my way straight
In the morning.

Hallelujah, Hallelujah, Hallelujah

In the morning, deep calls to deep
In the morning, You quietly speak
In the morning, You find those who seek
In the morning.

A former professor at Moody Bible Institute, Dr. Johnson is currently the associate pastor of Greater Pleasantview Baptist Church in Brentwood, Tennessee, and the dean of Franklin Bible Institute. Throughout his distinguished career, Ben has also been actively involved in music ministry around the world, performing in many different countries. Ben's two greatest spiritual passions are prayer and worldwide missions. His dedication to these two passions is evident in the devotions he has penned for this book.

The First Priority
Psalm 5:3

REV. BENJAMIN W. JOHNSON, SR., D.D.

*I*f we are to get the most out of our lives while we are still here on earth, it is very important to have specific, well-planned priorities for our daily lives. One of the most important of those priorities, if we want to be pleasing to God, is that we spend time with Him every morning.

You are very important to God. Each one of us is a masterpiece of God's amazing grace and there are no carbon copies! Each one of us is a love-gift from God the Father to God the Son. He loves us and wants to be with us every moment of our lives. He anticipates that we would also want to spend time with Him. Is that true for you?

What could be a higher priority than to take time to meditate on what God has done and what He means to us?

"Through Jesus, therefore, let us continually offer to God a sacrifice of praise—the fruit of lips that confess his name" (Hebrews 13:15). Yes, early in the day, we should be praising God. This is how we should fill our mornings!

How wonderful it is to know that God the Father desires to know us intimately. This intimate knowledge comes through His Son. "Now this is eternal life: that they may know you, the only true God and Jesus Christ, whom you have sent" (John 17:3). What a blessed verse this is to ponder at the beginning of our day.

An important part of our morning activity should be some time specifically set aside for worshiping God. He is worthy of our taking time to worship Him. "Come, let us bow down in worship, let us kneel before the LORD our maker" (Psalm 95:6). When we worship Him, it is easy to commune with Him. He wants us to take time to share His heart with us and wants us to share our hearts with Him. We were created to have eternal communion with God, yet in reality we usually spend very little time with Him. He wants our communion *now*, here on earth. Therefore, we should examine our lives.

You are VERY IMPORTANT *to God*

What are your priorities? How much time do you actually spend in intimate communion with your Heavenly Father?

It would be good for us to make a covenant with our Lord to start our days in communion with Him. The apostle

Paul is a good example for us to consider. "I want to know Christ and the power of his resurrection and the fellowship of sharing in his sufferings, becoming like him in his death," he wrote (Philippians 3:10). Paul yearned to be intimate with Christ because He was the center of Paul's life. "For to me, to live is Christ and to die is gain" (Philippians 1:21). Can you imagine what his times with the Lord must have been like?

Still, our Lord Jesus is the best model for praying. "Very early in the morning, while it was still dark, Jesus got up, left the house and went off to a solitary place, where he prayed" (Mark 1:35). It is good to have a definite place to pray, so that others will know that your praying time is important to you. Prayer is, in fact, the most important ministry that God gave to men. It needs to be taken seriously. It is more demanding than most Christians realize. Many believers take it too lightly, not realizing the tremendous preparation that we should put forth to pray to our eternal, holy, Heavenly Father. He is an awesome, incomprehensible God, but He made Himself known to us by our Lord and Savior, Jesus Christ.

"No eye has seen, no ear has heard, no mind has conceived what God has prepared for those who love him" (1 Corinthians 2:9). Imagine a man who lived in a coal mine most of his adult life and was taken to Hawaii and experienced the physical beauty of that island. Then, imagine that he had to come back to the coal mine and try to describe it in his coal mine vocabulary. This is the struggle we face when we try to contemplate all the greatness of God. Without biblical study, we have a very shallow concept of our triune

God. Therefore, Bible study should be added to prayer as part of our morning priority.

We must take time to get to know God in order to talk with people about Him. "If you remain in me and my words remain in you, ask whatever you wish and it will be given you" (John 15:7). This verse tells us that we must maintain unceasing communion with our triune God. Perhaps the best place to begin, our first priority, is to seek God in the morning with prayer and with study of His Word.

What could be more important?

New Beginnings
Genesis 28:18

REV. BENJAMIN W. JOHNSON, SR., D.D.

When we first open our eyes in the morning and take a brief moment to meditate, what a blessing it is to know that our Heavenly Father is watching over us. What a realization! Every morning is a new chance. Each day is a new opportunity to begin again. We can forget about yesterday's failures. We can be clean and new in the eyes of our Heavenly Father.

When we go to God in prayer each morning, the whole day has a fresh start. We can anticipate experiencing blessing, a clear mind for new ideas, and answers to yesterday's problems that are still not solved. We should ask our Father to help us in the morning, not just wait until we are mired down in another messy day.

Why not start our morning with a hallelujah shout, and then sing a song of praise to the Lord Jesus? It would energize our lungs and throats. The psalmist tells us to do it. "Shout for joy to the LORD, all the earth. Worship the LORD with gladness; come before him with joyful songs" (Psalm 100:1,2). Instead of complaining and worrying, let's lift our voices and sing.

The Bible tells of many people who experienced a new or fresh beginning with the Lord. They had different backgrounds and circumstances, yet they all were certain that the Lord heard their voices when they cried out in prayer. We can learn from them; they prayed to God without doubting. Paul wrote to young Timothy with this exhortation, "I want men everywhere to lift up holy hands in prayer, without anger or disputing" (1 Timothy 2:8). When we lift our voice in prayer, God forgives our sins and grants us a new start.

Jacob knew the importance of meeting with God in the early hours of the day. "Early the next morning Jacob took the stone he had placed under his head and set it up as a pillar and poured oil on top of it" (Genesis 28:18). Jacob had been on his way to Paddan Aram to get a wife. As night approached, he stopped to sleep. He took a stone and used it as a pillow. As he slept, God visited him in a dream. When he awoke, he knew that the Lord had visited him. Something powerful had occurred.

In the morning, he took the stone, poured oil upon it, and called the place "Bethel." He knew that after this encounter with God, his life would never be the same. And it wasn't. He renewed his vows to the Lord and continued his journey. We can learn a good lesson from this experience in Jacob's life. Although he made wrong decisions that affected his future life, he realized that God would forgive him and give him a brand new start. Isn't that what we all seem to need from time to time? We should take time with our Father and our Lord Jesus Christ and confess the wrongs we have done, deal with them honestly, and make necessary restitution. He will forgive us and let us begin again.

God, who is merciful, gracious, and patient looks beyond our faults and sees our needs! Hallelujah! Amen! He will hear us whenever we cry, "Lord, I am sorry!" As soon as He hears, He will answer. As Peter exhorts us: "Cast all your anxiety on him because he cares for you" (1 Peter 5:7).

In the MORNING, YOU make my way straight

Surely one of the greatest promises God offers us is that He will give us a new start, even when we have failed Him and fallen into the same sinful patterns again and again. His mercies are new every morning and His heart is stretched out toward us. Every day can be a new day and a new beginning. "Yet give attention to your servant's prayer and his plea for mercy, O LORD my God. Hear the cry and the prayer that your servant is praying in your presence this day" (1 Kings 8:28).

Preparation for Prayer
Jeremiah 29:13

REV. BENJAMIN W. JOHNSON, SR., D.D.

s we read and study the Bible, we realize that many of God's people met with Him early in the morning. If we have a good day, it is usually because we had a good morning. If we had a good morning, it is because we had a good beginning. If we had a good beginning, it is probably because we began our day with God.

In the Old Testament, the priests prepared and prayed early in the morning as a spiritual sacrifice. We should use them as a model and do the same thing early in the day. Is it possible that our Father and our Lord Christ Jesus may be challenging you to an intense prayer life? After all, God makes the same promise to us as He made to Jeremiah: "You will seek me and find me when you seek me with all your heart" (Jeremiah 29:13). Isn't this what we really want? If so,

I want to share with you six spiritual activities that will help to prepare you for this kind of prayer life.

1. Confession. We should prepare ourselves to enter into a time of prayer with confession of our sins. When we go to God in sincerity, we will confess our sins, and He will prepare us to be acceptable in His presence. Sometimes, we may have done something that we think is so bad that God cannot accept or forgive us. Don't believe this: It's Satan's lie. Believe what God says! "If we confess our sins, he is faithful and just and will forgive us our sins and purify us from all unrighteousness" (1 John 1:9).

You will SEEK ME AND find me

2. Thanksgiving. "Do not be anxious about anything, but in everything, by prayer and petition, with thanksgiving, present your requests to God" (Philippians 4:6). Our Heavenly Father does not want us to be "bent out of shape" spiritually. We should not let our sorrow, problems, and pain rob Him of hearing our voices raised in praise and thanksgiving to Him. In the morning, we do not want to find ourselves in the place of cheating God of what is due Him. Regardless of all our tears and concerns, we should give thanks to our Father and our Lord Christ Jesus with joyous singing.

3. Praise. "Through Jesus, therefore, let us continually offer to God a sacrifice of praise—the fruit of lips that confess his name" (Hebrews 13:15). Our lips were made to

major on praise and minor on sorrow. "O Lord, open my lips, and my mouth will declare your praise" (Psalm 51:15).

4. Worship. "Ascribe to the LORD the glory due his name. Bring an offering and come before him; worship the LORD in the splendor of his holiness" (1 Chronicles 16:29). He is wonderful, resplendent, magnificent, majestic! We are lost for adjectives when we try to adequately describe Him. But let us try!

5. Communion. "When they saw the courage of Peter and John and realized that they were unschooled, ordinary men, they were astonished and they took note that these men had been with Jesus" (Acts 4:13). When we spend time with God daily, we change in ways that people notice. It becomes obvious that we are on intimate terms with God. This is the most powerful kind of witness!

6. Fellowship. "We proclaim to you what we have seen and heard, so that you also may have fellowship with us. And our fellowship is with the Father and with his Son, Jesus Christ" (1 John 1:3). Remember, we were created by the triune God for fellowship. He desires fellowship with us. It is out of this fellowship that the most powerful prayers will arise.

Let us, then, follow the example of our Lord Jesus. "Very early in the morning, while it was still dark, Jesus got up, left the house and went off to a solitary place, where he prayed" (Mark 1:35). Our Lord led the way in showing us how to best spend our mornings. We can safely assume that He always met with the Father before He spent time with the disciples. Would it not please God if we were to do the same? Prepare yourself for prayer, and commit to spending your first morning hours in communion with the Lord. It will change the way you experience your day.

Waiting in Expectation

Psalm 46:10

REV. BENJAMIN W. JOHNSON, SR., D.D.

To start our day properly means to get our hearts set in the right direction for the day. It means giving the first moments of each new morning to God, which puts us in the place we need to be in for the whole day. Our first moments of the day can be moments of worry and stress, but this is not the way we should begin them. Instead, we should follow the scriptural exhortation: "Be still, and know that I am God; I will be exalted among the nations, I will be exalted in the earth" (Psalm 46:10). In the early hours of the morning, our hearts need to learn to "be still."

What does it mean to "be still"? When I glance through my commentaries, I find a number of helpful explanations. All of these are worth pondering:

Cease from murmuring.
Cease from laboring.
Cease from exerting yourself.
Leave matters with God.
Don't be anxious.
Trust in God's ability to control everything
and everybody.

All these are good advice when it comes to being "still."
Ultimately, the reason why we can be still is that we know
He is God. He is the source of all power, knowledge, goodness, justice, and truth. When we take time early in the
morning to meditate on His Word and seek Him in prayer,
we can find refreshment, a quieting of our inner struggles,
and a lasting peace.

When we still our hearts and lives, we open ourselves up
for communion with God and can expect that He will meet
with us at the point of our need. There are many examples in
the Bible of believers who waited for God with expectation.
Gideon, for example, waited in expectation for God's promise
(Judges 6:11-24).

When we pray, we should have "great expectations" to
hear from our Father. We should pray as David did, and
believe that God will answer our prayer, "Show me your ways,
O LORD, teach me your paths; guide me in your truth and
teach me, for you are God my Savior, and my hope is in you
all day long" (Psalm 25:4,5).

As the song says, "In the morning, I listen and wait." This
is the attitude with which we should start our day. "Wait for
the Lord; be strong and take heart and wait for the Lord"

(Psalm 27:14). "Be still before the Lord and wait patiently for him; do not fret when men succeed in their ways, when they carry out wicked schemes" (Psalm 37:7). David teaches us that we must first be still, then wait patiently before the Lord. We should be still and expectant.

Part of becoming still is to set aside some time to think about who it is we are talking to and waiting before. Yes, we must be reverent with God and with our Lord Christ Jesus. Then we can expect to hear from Him. "My soul waits for the Lord," wrote David, "more than the watchmen wait for the morning" (Psalm 130:6). Our Lord Jesus desires for us not only to wait, but to thirst for Him. "As the deer pants for streams of water, so my soul pants for you, O God" (Psalm 42:1).

Expectation gives birth to anticipation. "In the morning," the song says, "faith anticipates." Our attitude should be to trust in the faithfulness of our triune God. We can be confident that He will be faithful to fulfill His promises. "Now faith is the substance of things hoped for, the evidence of things not seen" (Hebrews 11:1 NKJV). Faith is the anticipation that God will do what He has said.

Each and every morning we should set our hearts in God's direction. We should still our restless minds, expecting that God will meet with us when we take the time to meet with Him. Each and every morning, it is the triune God's desire for us to spend time with Him. When we do this, each day can be lived in anticipation as we give God the first moments of the new morning. "Awake, my soul! Awake, harp and lyre! I will awaken the dawn" (Psalm 57:8).

LORD OF THE DAWN

Words by Scott Roley
and Phil McHugh

Music by Scott Roley

We're thankful for the rising sun,
For warmth and hope in the breaking dawn
For mercy, grace, and creation's song
To know we have only begun
Giving thanks to the Lord of the Dawn.

We're thankful for life that's full
That every hour You control
For the powerful way Your light breaks forth
To know we have only begun
Giving thanks to the Lord of the Dawn.

Lord of the Dawn, shine Your light
Chase the darkness where fear dims our sight
Make one more new day bright
Lord of the Dawn.

We praise You for Your steadfast love
From morning's light till the setting sun
Every moment Your eternity comes
To know we have only begun
Giving thanks to the Lord of the Dawn.

Lord of the Dawn, shine Your light
Chase the darkness where fear dims our sight
Make one more new day bright
Lord of the Dawn.

Lord of the Dawn every day
You take doubting and darkness away
Forever we give You the praise
Lord of the Dawn.

Scott Roley is associate pastor of Christ Community Church in Franklin, Tennessee, and heavily involved in community outreach. A musician, he has recorded with others as well as under his own name. Scott believes in living out his social concerns. He recently moved his family into one of the most underprivileged parts of Franklin in order to minister more effectively to an often overlooked part of the community. Scott is a man who believes in the power of God to change lives, as you'll see in the devotions he now shares.

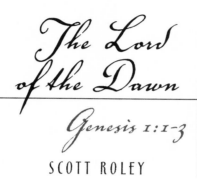

The Lord of the Dawn

Genesis 1:1-3

SCOTT ROLEY

"In the beginning God."

There is so much contained in these simple words. These are words that can strike fear in the heart of the unbeliever as their carnal mind first glimpses the reality of the Creator's power and presence. These same words are like a drink of pure water to the thirsty soul of the person of faith. And God not only exists, but He also has a purpose for our lives. This purpose, though sometimes hidden, is not altogether a secret. In the Genesis account we learn that God has initiated all things by His decree and that His purpose will be fulfilled in His own timing. He created everything out of nothing, and yet He makes Himself known to us. His name—*God*—is a noun which is plural in the original Hebrew text. We know from the rest of the Scriptures that God reveals Himself as Father, Son, and Spirit. Therefore, these simple opening words lead us immediately to a posture of worship!

The creation is sustained and held together by God's Word and Spirit. The chaos of nothingness and darkness is overcome by the eternal presence of God. As His Spirit moves, everything is made different. If He were to remove His Spirit, all of creation would return to chaotic darkness. Even our day-to-day life reflects this truth. Our lives are sustained and held together by Jesus' love and His commitment to us. How amazing this love truly is! As Lord of the Dawn, He ushers in each new day with love.

Interestingly, the Lord of the Dawn is also Lord of the Night. His control over all things cannot be questioned, and His sovereign rule over creation can never be interrupted. Knowing that He speaks each new dawn into existence is a great comfort for those who have the spiritual eyes to see. Each day breaks forth and chases the darkness away. This continuing cycle is God's way of showing us that, though we claim to see so well, without God's light there would only be darkness.

The great light shining in our hearts comes to us because God has spoken to us by His Word. Our trust is in Jesus, who is not only the Word made flesh, but also the light of the world. He illuminates every area of our life, revealing our sin and bringing us to maturity as we walk in the light. True maturity comes from a recognition of our sin and true repentance on a daily basis, even as the light of Christ exposes our darkness. Our inner darkness can be seen in both our dark thoughts and our dark deeds.

The fact that there is a God who is speaking to us means that there is a true relationship between Himself and His creation, a relationship of listening and responding and communicating with one another. The Genesis account shows us that it is God who initiates this relationship with His creation. He extends Himself to us, His creatures, in a true dialogue, with the give and take that accompanies real love. This love relationship can be seen even more clearly in Jesus, the Word of God, the one in whom the wisdom of God dwells and who is Himself God in the flesh.

It is so appropriate that light was the first creation of God, as it is the way that the beauty of creation is unveiled and the ultimate power of God manifested. In the Genesis story of creation, light is created even before the sun and moon. This is not by accident or some sort of scientific mistake. We are prone to think that without the sun, moon, and stars that life could not exist. But what we see is that God in His power and wisdom demonstrates by the very order of creation that He alone holds the life-giving light which He lends daily to the sun, the moon, and the stars. We can live without the heavenly bodies, but we cannot live without the light. I sometimes think of the sun or moon as the way we feel the reach of God's love. His love is extended to us as He lights the sky and takes away the darkness. Sometimes when I am far away from my loved ones, I remind them to look for the sun and moon, knowing that I can also see them from where I am. As we look together upon the powerful light of God's love, we are reminded of our union with Him and our love for each other.

We should surrender ourselves to this powerful and loving God. We should praise Him and thank Him for providing light in the midst of great darkness. Because of our sinful nature, our tendency is to walk away from our loving Father and to love the darkness instead of the light. Gratitude towards God saves us from the peril of embracing the darkness, mistakenly thinking it can give us life.

We're THANKFUL FOR THE *rising sun*

Moses, who was the author of the book of Genesis, knew the power of the Creator God. He experienced it in his own life as he struggled to believe God would indeed save him and his people. But the Lord of the Dawn shone on Israel in the midst of the Egyptian captivity, and God's light led them to the Promised Land. As we read of the creation today, we should be reminded to live as those who see, not with eyes lit by the false light of our idols, but as believers trusting in the Word of God, Jesus. By His powerful and life-giving light, He overcame the darkness, and He lit up all of creation so we might truly see. This is a truth we can experience every day of our life on earth, and then for all eternity. Thanks be to the Lord of the Dawn!

Sleeper, Awake!

Ephesians 5:8-14

SCOTT ROLEY

ake up, O sleeper, rise from the dead and Christ will shine on you." These words, which conclude this passage from Ephesians, were probably part of a hymn sung by the early church. They speak to us of Christ, the Lord of the Dawn, who awakens us from our slumber. Isn't it amazingly appropriate that this particular passage in Paul's letter to the "saints in Ephesus" should contain and conclude with an ancient hymn fragment? For what we are promised is such a great gift that it should cause our heart to sing! The promise of this ancient hymn speaks to every aspect of our spiritual slumber.

We are asleep in our sins. We sleep spiritually, dead in our sins until our precious Savior saves us. It may help to think of ourselves not only as asleep, but as drowning, with no ability to rescue ourselves. What we need is not merely the hand of a friend from the side of the pool, but a wonderful, merciful Savior, who dives into the tank to pull us out of the dark water. He finds us on the bottom; lungs filled with water, no breath, no pulse, no life. Then He hauls us to the surface and purposefully and skillfully does His work to resuscitate us. His breath breathes new life into us. His blood brings pulse and power to our hearts. He calls and we respond. He revives and saves us. We are awakened from death's sleep to a rebirth in the Spirit. We rise with Jesus from death's grip to our full heavenly reward.

Another image related to slumber is the light of Christ which awakens us each new morning. When we rise each day it is really a powerful and miraculous thing, a wonder we often overlook. We do not deserve life; it is given by God's grace. We should be thankful enough to say, "Lord, thank You for waking me and giving me another day!"

The sleeper in our passage can also be thought of in the context of one who is spiritually distracted by their sin. Romans 13:11,12 makes reference to this kind of sleep. It tells us that now is the time to wake up from our slumber: "The night is nearly over, the day is almost here." The idea of putting aside the deeds of darkness is contrasted with putting on "the armor of light." In our passage from Ephesians we are reminded that we were once darkness. As sinners we were in total darkness and our behavior was thoroughly depraved. Now, we are "light in the Lord." This is the reality brought about by the sanctifying work of Jesus. As light, we are thoroughly justified. All of

God's righteous wrath has been satisfied in the saving work of Christ on the cross. We are free to live in obedience to our loving, light-giving Father, who calls us into the marvelous light of His Son, the Lord Jesus Christ.

We who were orphaned children are now God's adopted children. As "children of light" we bear a resemblance to our Heavenly Father, who by His Spirit bears fruit in His children. This "fruit of the light," as Paul reminds us, consists in "all goodness, righteousness and truth." It is an awesome thing to understand that God is the loving Father who wakes His children so purposefully and carefully each and every morning with the purpose of creating in them His own characteristics: goodness, holiness, and truth.

Now, we ARE LIGHT IN the Lord

Jesus chases away all our darkness and doubt. Our fear often arises from unbelief. But when Jesus shines His light, the truths we tend to be blind to become visible and give us the hope that banishes fear. His power and strength are revealed, as well as the powerlessness of fear and doubt. We are often tempted to hide in the darkness, pretending that it is our friend. When we are confronted with the light of Jesus, we see that darkness can never be our friend. God's light conquers our despair and by it we see the goodness of our God.

When Paul writes, "everything becomes visible," he means *everything*. So ask yourself: What areas of my life remain hidden? We must remember that they can only be hidden from others, not from God. The best response to having our sins brought to light is to confess them, so that we might taste and see God's love in His act of forgiveness. Surely such grace awakens worship within our soul.

My greatest sin is to stay in my slumber. I must understand that all of God's warnings and rebukes are signs of His tender care and should lead me to repentance. How foolish it would be to stay in the darkness, fumbling with my self-contempt and fear. Instead, I should remember that I am an adopted son of the living God. What a privilege! I am forgiven for all my sins because of the work of Christ on my behalf. It is only when I boldly turn to Jesus that I can dance in the face of all my doubts and fears. I am awakened from my slumber and made able to respond to God's call. He is the gentle and all-powerful Father, the one who rescues me from the sleep of sin, so that today, tomorrow, and into all eternity, I will shine with the light of the Lord of the Dawn.

The Light of forgivenss

1 John 1:5-10

SCOTT ROLEY

God's grace and mercy are evident in His glorious creation and in His marvelous providence. But in nothing are they as evident as in the forgiveness He offers for our sin. We know God's mercy is real because we have experienced it poured out upon us. We still struggle with sin, but we have His assurance that we are forgiven because of what Christ has done for us.

Because we are sinners, we constantly battle with the temptation to convince ourselves that we are not really sinners! This war rages within us continually—either we agree with God and say, "Yes, I do sin" or we qualify and justify, redefining our sin as "failings," "mistakes," or "bad decisions." We often don't take them seriously enough. But God does. They sent Jesus to the cross on our behalf. His death was the payment for our sins. Sometimes we even disagree with the Lord's view of our nature and try to convince Him (and ourselves) that we really aren't all that bad. Our libertinism and perfectionism collide.

Flannery O'Connor once made the profound observation that "we avoid Jesus by avoiding sin." Only sinners need a Savior. Everyone else can get by on their own. Jack Miller has helped me see that the sin of saying we are "not sinning" manifests itself in both lack of faith (unbelief) and self-centered arrogance (pride). When I have this attitude, I may give lip service to the idea that Jesus loves me, but do I really believe it? Do I really believe that I'm so bad that someone, namely Jesus, would have to die for my sins? If we are honest with ourselves, I think we must admit that the sin of thinking we are "not sinning" is a temptation we all face.

The only answer for this dilemma comes from realizing that "God is light." His light exposes all our darkness and reveals the power and truth found only in fellowship with God. The light of Jesus, as the Lord of the Dawn, shines into our hearts and shows us to be what we truly are: needy, broken, and fragile people who are pretending that we are okay. It reveals us to be sinners who need a Savior. But the light also brings the peace of God, so that we are not overcome by grief when we see our sin for what it really is. This is the peace that is made real for us by the death of Jesus on the cross. It is a peace that has been bought by a price. Jesus spilled His blood as a substitute for our deserved death. We can't die for our own salvation.

What we must do is respond to the light that has shone on us and blink open our sleep-filled eyes to glimpse the grace and mercy extended to us by our Creator. God created us to have this kind of fellowship with Him, and our souls will not rest until we have it.

The light and peace of fellowship with God are entered into by faith, when we become convinced that His greatness and goodness empower Him to forgive *every* sin. Because we know this to be true, we can confess our sins freely. Because of Jesus, we see ourselves as weak and broken sinners. It's good for us to see ourselves with this kind of realism. It's exactly what God desires and requires of us. He wants us to be truthful and to lay down the pretense that somehow we've got it all together.

To be weak is to be strong because, when I know I am weak, I know I need Jesus. He does for me what I cannot do for myself. He takes my sins upon Himself and forgives them because His death and life were a substitution for me. I can rejoice because I am now clean and able to live with joy by the Holy Spirit. This joy overflows into fellowship with God and all those I come in contact with. This is what life should look like when it is lived in the light of Christ. We admit the reality of our sinful state, but we glory in the light of God's forgiveness.

The Lamb Is the Light

Revelation 21:22-27

SCOTT ROLEY

evelation 21 contains a beautiful description of heaven. There we will need no secondary light, such as the sun or moon, for the Lamb of God is Himself the lamp that gives light to the city. In his vision of the new Jerusalem, John, the beloved apostle, sees a scene whose brilliance is nearly too much for his human eyes. It is truly spectacular, a city that looks nothing like the cities we see today. This renewed city makes the combined beauty of San Francisco, Capetown, London, Paris, Tokyo, and New York pale in comparison. John's elaborate description of the precious gems and priceless jewels used by God in constructing the heavenly city stirs us and invites us. As we read, we long to see, to touch, and to live in such a remarkable place. Harvey Conn, a professor at Westminster

Seminary, reminds us that "it all started in a garden, but it all ends in a city. We have an urban future!"

This vision of the new Jerusalem surely moves every heart that truly trusts in Jesus. We often lose sight of this glorious future because we get swept up by all the clamoring business of our daily lives. But when we dream about our future home, the central theme that John desires for us to understand is that at the center of town, right in the heart of the city, the big deal, the main thing on Main Street, is the Lord Jesus Christ Himself! He is the Lamb of God, the Bridegroom for the bride, the Son of God, the Creator, and the Redeemer. In the New City His light shines so brightly that there is no need for the sun or the moon to shine on it. The glory of the Lord gives it light and the Lamb of God is its lamp.

Jesus, the Lamb of God, is the One who meets every need. He is in perfect control of all that happens. The city needs no light, because Jesus shines so perfectly. The city needs no temple as a place for worship, because Jesus is always visible and present. The incarnate Lamb of God is now the temple, the place of true worship. What a remarkably powerful image this is! Can any one of us really comprehend this idea? Sometimes we forget that Jesus is the center of everything in our lives. He who is at the center of the new city and at the Father's right hand is deserving of nothing less than our complete allegiance. Why would we refuse today to bend our knee to the King of Heaven, knowing that one day every person created from all time will bow their knee and confess with their tongue that Jesus is the Lord? This revelation of

Jesus should lead us to the posture of true faith—surrendered to the Lord Jesus Christ.

This is the ultimate posture of all nations: Every people and ethnic group will be represented around the throne of God. They will praise Him for His greatness and for creating His people with such diversity. This is all the more reason for us to celebrate the diversity of God's people on earth now. Remember the words from the Lord's Prayer, "on earth as it is in heaven." The unity of God's people is a part of the gift of warmth and hope we can find in each new day's dawn. Let's not wait for heaven to learn to truly love one another! Each time we place the needs of a brother or sister before our own, or cross over racial, social, denominational, and cultural barriers to reach out, we experience a taste of the heavenly city to come. But even then, we are only scratching the surface of the depth, width, height, and length of Jesus' love.

This love is a love that will never end. The gates of the new Jerusalem will never be closed, never locked up for the night, and no watchman will be needed. They say that New York City is "the city that never sleeps." But it is only a dim reflection of the true city that never sleeps—the new Jerusalem!

If we want to be a part of the new city God is constructing for us, we need to make sure that our names are written in the Lamb's book of life. We must believe in Jesus as the Son of God, who was slain for sinners and resurrected as the Lamb of God, the One who takes away the sins of the world. Jesus is the Savior of the world and He has many names. Not only is He the Lamb of God, He is also the Good Shepherd. As the Lamb, He lays down His life for His people. As the

Shepherd, He knows the names of each one of His lambs. The names in the Lamb's book of life are secured because of His power to save. Each name is mysteriously included in the resurrected life of Jesus. This union with Christ is among the most powerful of all biblical images. Because of Jesus' sinlessness, we who are included in Him are cleansed and made fit for dwelling in the heavenly city. In that city there is no shame or deceit. We can hold our heads up high, because the song we sing is to the praise of God and His glory. He is the focus of all our worship, and His city reflects His beauty and perfection. No wonder there is no need for any kind of secondary light sources. The only light needed is the brilliance of the Lamb who is the lamp.

MORNING STAR

*Words and Music
by Michael Card*

*T*his day is a desert, full of frights
Morning Star, O Morning Star
And I must cross it before the night
O Bright and Morning Star.

The day can be too much for me
Morning Star, O Morning Star
Be Thou my vision so I can see
O Bright and Morning Star
Bright and Morning Star.

Come rise and shine
In Your holiness
O radiant Son of Righteousness
And warm Your people
Both near and far
And shine through me
O Morning Star
Shine through me
O Morning Star.

Now like a beacon come and blaze
O Morning Star, Morning Star
Lead on Good Shepherd through the maze
O Bright and Morning Star
Bright and Morning Star.

Your compassion's new every morning
It fills us up so we can sing
So we sing.

Michael Card is one of the most respected and recognized voices in Christian music, known for his commitment to creativity and biblical authority. His books and albums have sold millions of copies and won many prestigious awards. Michael's passions in life include his family, biblical study, Celtic culture, and motorcycles. As these essays show, he is also one of the best storytellers around.

One Morning on the Shore

John 21:4-12

MICHAEL CARD

It was getting to be late in the evening when Peter announced, "I'm going fishing. Who wants to go along?" The other disciples really didn't know exactly what to do. Of all the things Jesus had prepared them for, doing nothing wasn't one of them.

"We'll go with you," a few of them replied, wandering toward the lake as if they had no idea where they were off to. They set out just as the sun went down, washing the hills on the eastern side of the lake with a warm golden light.

The fishing was "off" that night. It seemed that no matter how many times they hauled in the nets, they were always empty. As the evening chill began to set in, they began to feel another kind of emptiness, an emptiness of heart and soul.

John, the youngest and most tenderhearted of them all, began reminiscing. "I remember another time when the fishing was bad, just like tonight. Remember, Peter? And Jesus asked us to go out again and you rolled your eyes and mumbled under your breath, 'What does a carpenter know about fishing?' Remember?"

Peter didn't answer because, though he could recall that morning with perfect clarity, he most certainly did not want to remember it now. He clearly remembered the sound of Jesus' voice that first time he heard it. That flat northern drawl that marked Him as a Nazarene. He remembered His ridiculous request to go out fishing again on a lake that had already proven itself empty of fish. He remembered the way the boat suddenly lurched to port as if someone had simply dumped the fish into the net from above. And he remembered looking down into the water and seeing more fish than he had seen in his entire life.

That morning, more than two years ago now, things had made perfect sense to Peter. *Here is a Messiah I can die for*, he had thought to himself. Never had he dreamed that Jesus would be the kind of Savior who would die for him instead. And later, when Jesus had laughed and said he would make them fishers of men, Peter had pictured an easy life ahead, like the easy and miraculous catch that morning. The warmth of that morning, so long ago, the full nets, everyone laughing together, and Jesus in the midst of them all, full of joy. How different this morning was. Cold, dark, with empty nets and hearts, lonely, joyless, and, above all, hungry. The disciples thought the night was never going to end. Their hands were shriveled and cold. Their backs ached from hauling in the nets time after time.

Peter was the first to spot the faint glow of sunrise, low in the east. The tired faces of his companions came into view as the gray sky above them became lighter. They made one final cast of the net and, of course, came up empty again.

"Steer for that fire on the shore," James told his little brother, pointing in the general direction.

About one hundred yards away they could barely make out the shadow of someone standing beside the fire. "Must be one of the women," someone muttered.

"Children, you haven't caught any fish, have you?" The voice was coming from the shadow beside the fire. There was a strange familiarity in its tone.

Peter was annoyed by the question, as well as by a stranger referring to them as children. He shouted back with an angry tone, "No, we haven't caught a thing."

"Try the starboard side," the shadow called back.

"Who does this person think he is?" Peter hissed, genuinely angry by now.

Without thinking, James and John tossed the net overboard. Suddenly the boat lurched to starboard and the ropes began to creak. The mast dipped dangerously close to the surface of the water. Without needing to hear James' command, they all leaned into the net's ropes and began hauling it in.

John was looking down into the water for the first sight of what the catch might be. When he saw that the net was full of fish he suddenly remembered that earlier morning and the first miraculous catch. He gasped and looked toward the shore. "It's the Lord," he whispered in excitement. Peter, hearing what John said, wrapped his cloak around him and dove into the water.

"What about...?" Nathanael blustered.

Though they had to pull in the net and set to their oars, the others in the boat reached the shore at the same time as Peter. Matthew sat in the bow excitedly counting the large fish.

Peter, James, and John were the first to reach the fire. They smelled the fish and bread before they even reached the beach, but now they saw them, steaming beside the coals. The person standing there seemed clothed in shadows. They could not quite make out his face but they knew it was Jesus, the Risen Lord.

There was no angelic host. No heavenly music. They were not commanded by a voice from heaven to fall down on the sand and worship Him. There was only the crackling of the fire, the smell of the fish and bread, and the silence of the One who stood beside them.

"Come, bring some of what you have caught," Jesus said to them. *Yes, it is His voice*, Peter thought. *Simple, welcoming, and warm. How like Him it is.* As Jesus took the fish from Nathanael's hand, the other three could see the scar in His wrist. John winced to see it.

"Does that hurt?" he asked with his usual innocence.

"No, not now." Jesus said, and for the first time they could make out His smile. Though He was the Risen Lord of Glory, He had come to them in simplicity. Though He might have met them in splendor, with an angelic host, He was there cooking breakfast for them. Jesus (the same yesterday, today, and forever) met His disciples that morning precisely as He had always met them; at the point of their need. He knew they were hungry. He knew they were unable to catch anything. And so, He prepared the fire, caught the fish, and made the bread, then waited for them as if He had nothing more important to do.

This very morning, the Risen Lord, the Lord of Glory, desires to spend breakfast with you and me. He waits for us as if He has nothing more important to do. Make the time for Him, even if it means swimming through a sea of business to get there.

Struggling in Prayer

Mark 1:35

MICHAEL CARD

Very early in the morning, while it was still dark, Jesus got up, left the house, and went off to a solitary place to pray. Simon and his companions went to look for Jesus, and when they found Him they exclaimed: "Everyone is looking for you!"

They had not been together with Jesus very long, perhaps only a month or so, but their ministry was going well. People's lives were touched and transformed. In Capernaum, everyone in the synagogue was impressed and amazed by Jesus' teaching. But when He cast the evil spirit out of the man who was possessed, they were even more in awe. The people couldn't stop talking about it. "What authority He has!" everyone exclaimed. "Where could this kind of authority possibly come from?"

The people flocked to see what it was all about and to see if Jesus could fulfill their most urgent requests. As a result, He had been up late into the night, healing everyone who came to Him for help. Mark goes so far as to suggest that everyone in town was there! Can you imagine the demands placed upon the Lord by this crowd of needy people?

There are different kinds of weariness. Sometimes the cure is to rest and sleep. Often we see Jesus doing just that. He knew when His body needed the refreshment of sleep. But there is another kind weariness; a weariness of the soul that only prayer can heal. That is the kind of weariness Jesus was fighting on this particular morning.

The Bible tells that He went to a "solitary place." But the text, literally, speaks of an *eremos topos*, a wilderness or desert place. Using this word gives us the sense not simply of His being alone, of finding solitude—but of being surrounded by the desolation and danger of the wilderness. Mark's Gospel tells us that during His temptation *in the wilderness* Jesus was "with the wild beasts" (1:13 NKJV). The place to which Jesus retreats for prayer is menacing and unsafe. It is a picture of the real world, unveiled. Jesus leaves the warmth of His bed and the companionship of His friends and wanders into the wilderness, seeking in the midst of it the familiarity of His Father. There are two points, it seems, that we can make of all this.

First, we should consider the nature of the One who rises so early to spend the morning in prayer. He is the Son of God, who bears the fullness of the image of the Father. He is the One who is always obedient, who always hears and does just what His Father tells Him to do. And yet, many times

He found it necessary to spend the entire night in prayer. His relationship with the Father was everything to Jesus. And prayer seems to be the foundation of that relationship. If it was so important for Jesus to spend large blocks of time in prayer, how much more should we be spending that kind of time speaking and, more importantly, listening to the Father.

Second, the fact that the wilderness was the place Jesus sought for prayer should tell those of us who seek only comfort and safety that God is best found and heard in the midst of terror and turmoil. We want to flee, to retreat to the sanctuary for prayer. And there is nothing wrong with that. But Jesus shows us there is more to prayer than comfort and security. There is also the wrestling in the wilderness with what sickens us and scares us to death. There is a struggle with God and His will for us that might indeed leave us limping like Jacob after the battle is over. But it is precisely the limp, the woundedness, that we may most need to experience and that the world most needs to see in us.

This morning God is calling us to come to Him in the desert, to meet with Him in the most arid place of our souls. He is asking us to follow and to find His Son there in the middle of the danger and turmoil that we know exists outside our door. He is inviting us to join, with Jesus, in the battle that is prayer. He invites us to take off the gloves, to lean into the fight with all we are. Only then can we stand alongside His Son as He sends us out to speak His Word and do His will.

The Morning Star

Revelation 22:16

MICHAEL CARD

In astronomy, the morning star is not a star at all, but actually the planet Venus. For a portion of the year, Venus appears early in the morning, just before sunrise, only to be overcome by the light of the sun as it moves behind our star in its orbit. During this time, it is referred to as the "morning star." Later, it can be seen just before sunset, going down early in the evening, hence the term "evening star." Venus is unmistakable, the third brightest object in the sky. Only the sun and moon outshine it.

"It is always darkest before the dawn," Thomas Fuller wrote in 1650. Nothing could be truer. While Venus is known as both the evening and the morning star, in Scripture the term "morning star" is the only one used in reference to Jesus. This is because it is in the morning that we most need light.

Despite the growing light of dawn, many times mornings can be the darkest time of the day. Sometimes it is not easy to find the courage to embrace all that lies before us in the new day. So many worries and fears can assail us in these early morning hours. We can find ourselves living in dread of the hours before us. To face the new day with joy requires a courage that must come from outside ourselves.

Jesus is three times referred to as the "Morning Star." Once by Peter and twice by John. Interestingly enough, these were two men who knew Him intimately.

Christ will DISPEL THE darkness

"I am the Root and the Offspring of David, and the bright Morning Star" (Revelation 22:16).

"I will also give him the morning star" (Revelation 2:28).

"And we have the word of the prophets made more certain, and you will do well to pay attention to it, as to a light shining in a dark place, until the day dawns and the morning star rises in your hearts" (2 Peter 1:19).

The Greek word that both Peter and John use is *phosphorous* or "light bearer." And while John is simply quoting what he heard Jesus say in his remarkable vision, Peter is putting together his own words (though also by Divine inspiration).

Peter is referring to that darkest of times just before the morning breaks. But the darkness he has in mind is the darkness of a world or a heart that does not know Jesus Christ. He trusts that the light of Christ will dispel all the darkness that encroaches upon the world. The first light he mentions is the light of prophecy. Those early prophetic words of expectation were like small candles shining against the massive weight of the darkness until the time of the Incarnation. But, says Peter, a time came for the world, and will hopefully come for each individual, when the Morning Star, the true Light Bearer, will rise on the horizons of our hearts. Then the darkness will be fully and finally and forever be pushed back and overcome.

If this is a dark morning for you, if you feel in need of light in your life, begin with this passage from the prophet. It represents a small flickering flame:

> I see Him, but not now,
> I behold Him, but not near
> A Star shall rise out of Jacob.
> —Numbers 24:17

Then listen to the simple words of the Morning Star, the true Light Bearer, and allow them to transform the darkness into a new morning for you:

> I am the Light of the World.
> He who follows Me will not walk in darkness,
> but will have the Light of Life.
> —John 8:12

Morning Worship

Job 38:6,7

MICHAEL CARD

"On what were its footings set, or who laid its cornerstone—while the morning stars sang together and all the angels shouted for joy?" (Job 38:6,7). There are a number of mysterious questions found in the Old Testament that look forward to Jesus as the answer. This question is addressed by God to His suffering and confused servant, Job. We know the answer, of course. It was through Jesus that God created everything. Jesus is the creative and sustaining Word of the Father. This conviction was a part of the earliest confession of the Church. We hear it echoed in the first chapters of John, Colossians, and Hebrews.

Upon the morning of creation, while the cornerstone of our world was being set into place, the Bible tells us that something special took place: "the morning stars sang together and the angels shouted for joy." (This may be an example of poetic repetition. The "morning stars" may be another term for angels, since angels are often referred to as stars in the Bible.) When our world first came into being, there was a visceral response from the host in heaven. They could not hold back their joyful shout, the song that leapt from their luminous lips. For them, seeing the world—our world—come into existence, witnessing its loving creation by the Word of God, was a musical moment. They could do nothing else but sing.

There is something deeply and almost primitively spiritual about singing. It is one of the few pursuits that human beings hold in common with creation. (Along with groaning, that is; see Romans 8:22.) The birds sing, as do the whales. Scientists tell us that their songs are unthinking responses arising from their evolutionary past. But I believe there is more to it than that. Whales and birds and even stars sing because of their essential participation in the Creation. The songs of whales and birds have recognizable patterns. They have *order*. The stars also resonate with predictable patterns of sound. They ring like enormous fiery bells. Why?

Because they, and the whales and birds and flowers and the very dust of the earth itself, fell from the fingertips of the Creator, and their only appropriate response to Him is worship. Their songs of worship spring, not from rational realization (for they are not thinking beings as we are), but from simply being part of the fabric of creation, a creation which bears upon it the intricate pattern of its Creator. They sing praise because they belong to creation. They have no choice.

But we do.

We are unique in the world in that we can say no. We can close our mouths and hearts (though it is the most unnatural thing in the world for us to do so) and refuse to recognize with our minds what the rest of creation knows without having to reason it out. In short, we can *choose*.

So then, choose this day whom you will serve. Choose this morning to whom the song of your life will be sung. To yourself? To the fallen world? Or to the One who lovingly created you with lips and tongue you can use to praise Him. Choose whether to remain dark and mute or to join with the birds and whales and every sort of shining creature, even with the stars themselves, to praise the One who created, who was born, who died, and who rose again so that the song might be sung, that the joyful shout might be shouted from *all* creation.

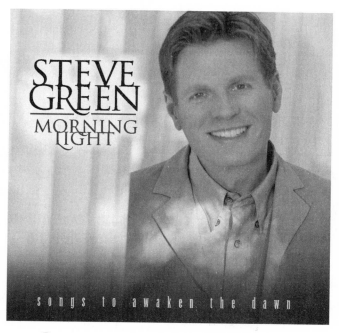

Treasure the Moment . . .

Morning Light—Songs to Awaken the Dawn offers up bright moments of praise in celebration of life and faith. In it Steve Green offers 12 deeply devotional songs that create a peaceful, heartfelt atmosphere of devotion and communion with the Savior.

Featuring songs such as "In the Morning," "Morning Has Broken," "Morning Star," and "All That You Say" with feature vocals by Twila Paris, *Morning Light—Songs to Awaken the Dawn* will be a welcome interlude anytime of the day.

Available on compact disc or cassette
wherever you buy Christian music.

SPARROW®

Song Credits

HE IS GOOD
Frank Hernandez/Jeff Nelson
© 1998 Birdwing Music/His & Hernandez Music (ASCAP).
All rights administered by EMI Christian Music Publishing.

IN THE MORNING
Steve Green
© 1999 Birdwing Music/Steve Green Music (ASCAP).
All rights administered by EMI Christian Music Publishing.

ALL THAT YOU SAY
Steve Green/Wes King
© 1999 Birdwing Music/Steve Green Music (ASCAP)/Sparrow Song/
Uncle Ivan Music (BMI). All rights administered by
EMI Christian Music Publishing.

I OFFER MYSELF
I WILL AWAKEN THE DAWN
Steve Green/Phil Naish
© 1999 Birdwing Music/Steve Green Music/Meadowgreen Music Company/
Davaub Music (ASCAP). All rights administered by
EMI Christian Music Publishing.

DOXOLOGY
(Public Domain—New music by Phil Naish)

BREATHE ON ME, BREATH OF GOD
Phil Naish
© 1999 Meadowgreen Music Company/Davaub Music (ASCAP).
All rights administered by EMI Christian Music Publishing.

MORNING HAS BROKEN
arr. Rob Mathes
Arrangement © 1999 River Oaks Music Company/
Maybe I Can Music (BMI).
All rights administered by EMI Christian Music Publishing.

LISTEN
Rob Mathes
© 1999 River Oaks Music Company/Maybe I Can Music (BMI).
All rights administered by EMI Christian Music Publishing.

MORNING STAR
Michael Card
© 1999 Mole End Music (administered by Word Music).

LORD OF THE DAWN
Scott Roley/Phil McHugh
© 1999 Scott Roley Music (administered by CMI).
All rights reserved.